Reflections
OF
WASHINGTON, D.C.

Reflections
OF
WASHINGTON, D.C.

Eleanor Berman

GALLERY BOOKS

Text
Eleanor Berman

Design
Marnie Searchwell

Photography
Robert Llewellyn

Photo Editor
Annette Lerner

Project Director
Sandra Still

CONTENTS

Above: *sunlight on the capital's plethora of government buildings.*
Right: *ripples on the Reflecting Pool, which leads down to the Washington Monument.*

Introduction

Washington, D.C. is a showcase for everything that is best about America. The nation's capital strikes newcomers today with its beauty, grace, and space, its great public monuments and leafy promenades. Twenty million visitors from around the globe arrive each year, not only to transact official government business but also to admire, to learn about the nation's history and heritage, and to visit some of its most spectacular cultural institutions.

This is a capital built to human scale. Unlike cities dense with skyscrapers, law has decreed that the highest points in the Washington landscape will always be the magnificent Capitol dome and the slim graceful shaft of the Washington Memorial. The low buildings let in the sunlight. The city is green with parks and promenades, squares and plazas. Much of the architecture is classic and timeless, beauty that has nothing to do with trends and fads.

For visiting Americans, there is pride in the beauty as well as the heritage these buildings represent, a new awareness of the country's purpose and its history – something every visitor feels in his own skin.

On the borderline of North and South, Washington is a blend of cultures and accents. The late President John F. Kennedy jokingly called it a city of southern efficiency and northern charm, but in fact there is

Above: *Independence Day fireworks light up the Capitol.*

plenty of warmth, and things do manage to get done, albeit at a gentle pace.

In many ways, Washington is a sampler of America. Among the population of more than three million, there is a constant infusion of newcomers, who have come from every part of the land to serve in Congress or work in the government. Along with the legislators come the lobbyists, the lawyers, and other power brokers hoping to influence national policy. Nearly half of the nearly 650,000 residents living in Washington's city limits are employed by government agencies, or base their occupations on serving or influencing the government in some way.

Adding to the city's flavor are diplomats from 150 countries, who represent their nations in the capital city where decisions are echoed in every capital in the world. The mix is healthy, keeping the city varied, vibrant, cosmopolitan.

Above: *fireworks blaze joyously amid crowds around the Reflecting Pool on July 4.*

Facing page: *the seventeen-foot-high bronze of General Grant silhouetted against the Capitol.*

History of the City

It is hard to believe that two hundred years ago, when this site along the Potomac River was chosen for the new nation's capital city, there was much argument. The year was 1790. In Congress, New Englanders, led by Alexander Hamilton of New York, wanted the capital in the North. Southerners, championed by Thomas Jefferson of Virginia, demanded it be placed in the South. The story goes that Hamilton and Jefferson struck a deal in which the federal government assumed the northern states' debts, and in return, it was agreed that the capital would be sited in the South.

Below: *leafless but bursting with blossom, the Japanese cherry trees for which Washington is famous herald the spring. The trees, a gift from the Japanese, are at their best in the Tidal Basin area.*

The actual site was chosen by the young nation's first president, George Washington, just a convenient eighteen-mile commute up the Potomac from his Mount Vernon home. On July 12, 1790, Washington signed an Act of Congress to fix Philadelphia as temporary capital until the first Monday in December, 1800, when the federal government would officially take up residence "in a district not exceeding ten miles square on the River Potomac."

Washington had chosen a site at the confluence of the east and west Potomac branches, between the ports of Georgetown, Maryland, and Alexandria, Virginia. Maryland and Virginia each donated the necessary land within the boundaries set (the Virginia land was later returned to the state). The nation faced the task of creating a new city upon these boggy lowlands beside the river.

The job of planning was given to Major Pierre Charles L'Enfant, a former member of Washington's Continental Army staff, who had distinguished himself by redesigning New York's Federal Hall in 1789. It was a happy choice. The Frenchman's design, inspired by Paris and Versailles, was brilliant, and as practical as

it was beautiful. L'Enfant envisioned 160-foot-wide
avenues radiating from scenic squares and circles that
would be adorned with monumental sculptures and
fountains. The avenues, to be named after the states,
would sweep through the city, allowing for easy
access to the center from every corner, and would
provide long majestic vistas to each circle and square.
The real show-stopper would be a mile-long,
400-foot-wide mall extending from the site of the
future Capitol building.

Though President Washington approved of both
the architect and his plan, L'Enfant apparently could
not get along with local land owners, who disputed
the sums the government offered for their property.
He was reluctantly dismissed in 1792. Refusing to
accept a token twenty-five hundred dollars for his
work, the planner sued Congress for one hundred
thousand dollars. It was a lost cause that left him
penniless, and L'Enfant died a pauper in 1825. In 1929,
as a belated token of the nation's appreciation, his
remains were moved from a little-known grave to
Arlington Cemetery.

Work began in the early 1790s on both the Capitol
and the President's House, but progress was slow.
When President John Adams and the Congress arrived
on schedule in December, 1800, both found
themselves moving into buildings that were still under
construction. The city itself was floundering. There
had been no rush to move to the new capital city.
There was no industry to attract settlers to this
marshy site; the only residents were government
employees and a few farmers.

*Above: winter grips the
Reflecting Pool, which
frequently freezes for weeks at
a time, forming a fine ice rink.*

*Right: Arlington Memorial
Bridge, completed in 1932. The
bridge connects the capital with
Arlington Cemetery.*

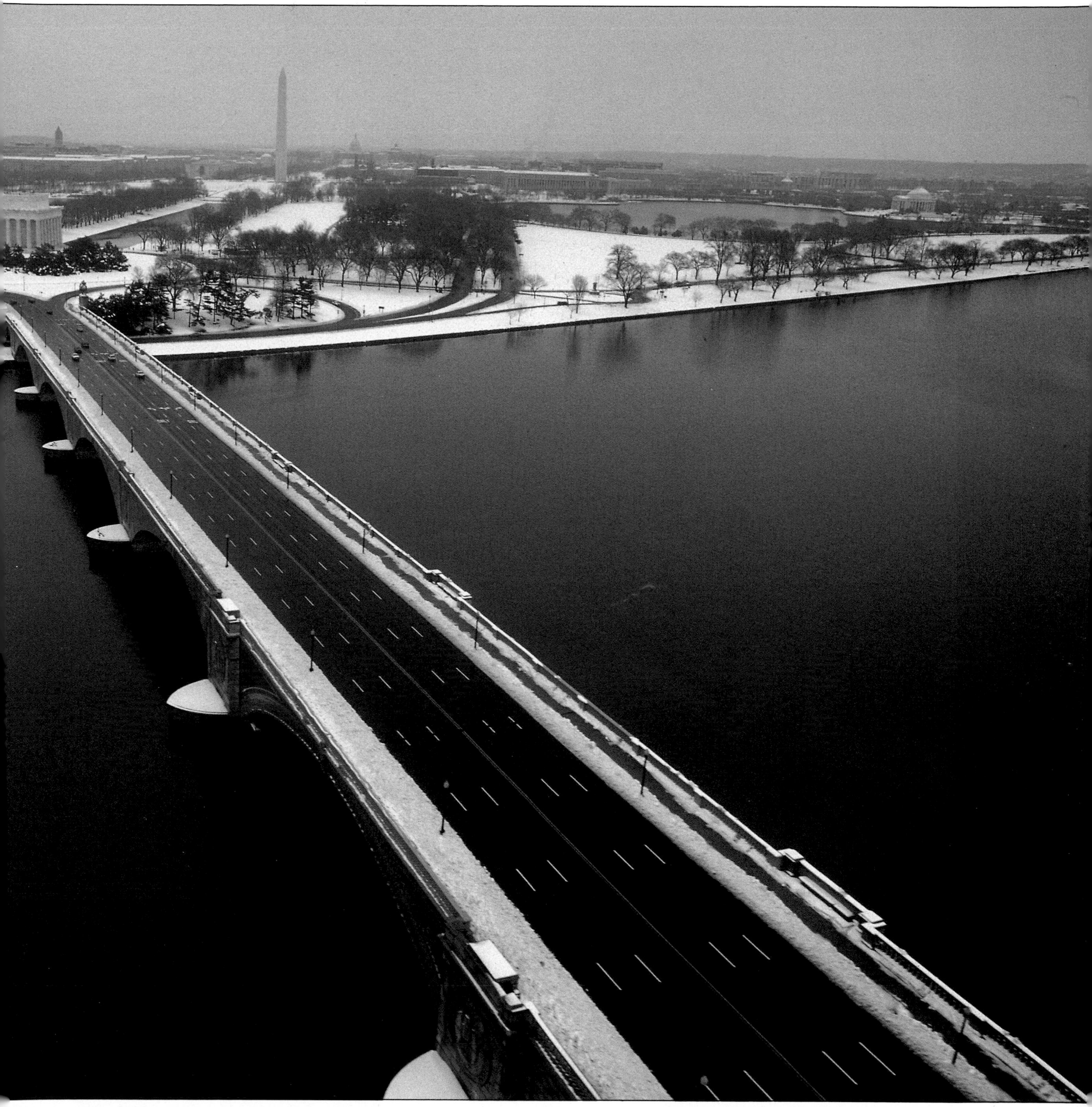

Left: *the Potomac River winding through the capital on its way to join the Atlantic in Chesapeake Bay.*

The new capital had a worse trial ahead, the War of 1812. British Rear Admiral Sir George Cockburn vowed that he would "make his bow" in President James Madison's drawing room. In August, 1814, the British did indeed invade and burn the President's House as well as the Capitol and the Library of Congress buildings.

Only an act of God saved Washington from total destruction. That night, a thunderstorm drenched the city and quenched the flames. Damage was so

Early sunshine lights the nation's Capitol and the Washington Monument, the highest buildings in the city.

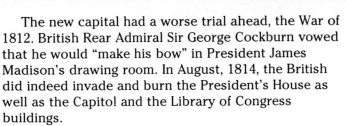

The cast-iron dome of the world-famous United States Capitol, designed to appear as white marble.

extensive, however, that a dismayed Congress discussed abandoning the city altogether. The motion was lost by only nine votes.

A New Beginning

Morale improved when repairs began and the charred President's mansion was re-painted sparkling white, to become known ever after as "The White House."

Congress, meanwhile, met in a hastily built brick structure, while Charles Bulfinch was appointed architect to oversee the construction of a new Capitol.

The struggling city was still not attracting new residents, however. In 1842, Charles Dickens described Washington as "spacious avenues that lead nowhere . . . public buildings that need but a public to be complete." Living in the city at that time was anything but pleasant. The stretch that is now stately Pennsylvania Avenue was then a bug-infested canal

that frequently flooded, leaving surrounding streets mired in mud. The mall that L'Enfant had envisioned as a grand avenue from the Capitol was a muddy, maloderous swampland. Washington was the butt of jokes. Legislators left their wives and families at home, and foreign ambassadors who were stationed here collected hardship pay during their terms.

It was the Civil War that turned the city's fortunes. President Abraham Lincoln's call to arms in 1861 brought thousands of Union soldiers to occupy Washington, almost doubling the population. Many of these people never left.

Lincoln also insisted that the construction underway for a new tiered dome on the Capitol building should continue. "If the people see the Capitol going on, it's a sign we intend the Union shall go on," he said. The dome was completed in 1863.

After the war, the city grew further as ex-slaves and war-weary soldiers settled in the area. Racial tensions arose as blacks grew to number one third of the population. Again, there was talk of moving the capital – to St. Louis, Chicago, or Kansas City.

But Washington won out once again, and the city began to hold its own. In 1867, Congress granted the District of Columbia territorial status, marking an important turning point. Boards of Public Works and Health were appointed. One man, Alexander Shepherd, a close friend of President Ulysses S. Grant, became vice president of the Board of Public Works and a one-man dynamo responsible for transforming the city. Under his guidance, the foul canal running through the city was finally filled. Sewers and sidewalks were built, unsanitary buildings condemned, streets paved, and sixty thousand trees planted. In 1874, Frederick Law Olmsted, the noted designer of New York's Central Park, began filling the Capitol grounds with rare trees, representative of different parts of the country. Today more than three thousand trees stand as shady tributes to Olmsted's plan.

Public buildings were going up in impressive numbers. The Library of Congress, Union Station, Corcoran and Renwick Galleries of Art, the Post Office, Treasury Building, National Portrait Gallery, and the first two Smithsonian buildings were completed. In 1884, the first great monument, the Washington Monument, finally was in place, after years of embarrassing delays. By the end of the nineteenth century, Washington was a metropolis to be reckoned with.

The Reflecting Pool, which is 2,000 feet long, is designed to reflect the Washington Monument and the Lincoln Memorial. Built in the 1920s, this stretch of water is now synonymous with the Monument.

Modern Washington

The first part of the twentieth century saw Washington's beauty emerge as it turned into a city of parks and gardens. A committee was formed in 1901 to develop the city's park system. Among those appointed were noted classical architect Charles McKim, landscape architect Frederick Law Olmsted, Jr., and sculptor Augustus Saint-Gaudens. They not only resurrected L'Enfant's plans, but extended his Mall design to stretch from the Capitol past the Washington Monument on to the Lincoln Memorial, giving the city a magnificent two-mile green centerpiece. The Botanic Gardens were created in 1902, and ten years later a gift of three thousand cherry trees came from the Japanese government as a token of friendship, a gift that has given the city legendary springtime beauty and its most famous annual festival.

The great depression of the 1930s brought massive new construction, as President Franklin D. Roosevelt's WPA program put thousands of jobless men to work building the "federal triangle" of office buildings. The Supreme Court and the Federal Reserve Building were

Virtually deserted highways in the snow form sweeping curves reminiscent of a monochrome abstract painting.

Foreshortening by a telephoto lens seems to bring the Capitol and the Washington Monument within yards of the Lincoln Memorial.

Above: *the Washington Monument. Finished in 1884, it predates the Lincoln Memorial by almost thirty years.*

Left: *a reflection of the dome of the Capitol, the bronze* Statue of Freedom *visible in the shimmering waters.*

Right: *cherry blossom frames the Jefferson Memorial in April, a building seen at its best at this time across the Tidal Basin.*

two of the structures that went up in this period.

Personalities and world events continued to shape the city. In 1941, Washington acquired its most important art institution when the National Gallery of Art opened its doors, a gift from Pittsburgh millionaire Andrew Mellon. Two more important structures were completed even as the nation was engaged in fighting World War II. Both the Jefferson Memorial and the Pentagon were finished in 1943.

A major performing arts center for the city had been talked about for decades; the tragic assassination of President John F. Kennedy in 1963 turned this dream to reality. Money and gifts poured

in from all quarters, including foreign governments, and the John F. Kennedy Center for the Performing Arts opened its doors in 1971, serving as both a memorial to the late president and a much needed cultural center.

The nation's Bicentennial was the occasion for the opening of the Smithsonian's Air and Space Museum, which is visited by more than eight million people each year, making it the city's most popular museum – and one of the most visited in the world. And more museums seem to open every year, with collections encompassing everything from African art to a salute to women's role in art history.

One of the newest of the nation's memorials is one of its most moving, the Vietnam Veterans Memorial, which was dedicated in 1982.

Recently, residential Washington has taken on a new look, as parks and promenades are being developed along the Potomac in Georgetown. Landmark buildings such as the Old Post Office and Union Station have become new gathering places, filled with shops and restaurants.

By the end of its second century, the nation's capital had moved from laughing stock to the forefront of the nation. Washington was at last what its founders had dreamed of creating, a world-class city.

Above: *sunny chrysanthemums around a pool in the White House grounds.*
Right: *the White House, cocooned by trees. Every President except George Washington has lived here at 1600 Pennsylvania Avenue.*

Washington's Great Buildings

Washington is filled with fine buildings, but three hold special places in the nation's history and affection. They are the cornerstones of the balance of power decreed by the Constitution, the homes of the chief executive, the Congress, and the Supreme Court.

The White House

Without doubt it is the "President's House," known the world over as the White House, that best reflects the human history of Washington, the lives and personalities of the presidents and their first ladies who have resided here, presiding over the nation's fortunes.

The only residence of a head of state open to the public on a regular basis free of charge, it is home, executive office, and a museum. Exhibits include fine antique furniture in period settings, historic memorabilia, a portrait gallery of America's presidents and first ladies, and works by some of the nation's finest artists.

Though he picked the location and hired the architect, George Washington never slept here. He died in 1799 before the building was completed.

Above: *a sated satyr peers into an elegant White House ewer.*

Washington and Thomas Jefferson, both amateur architects, held a contest for the design of the President's House to be built in the new federal city. It was to be a building of "size, form and elegance . . . looking beyond the present day."

James Hoban, an Irish architect and builder who had done work in Charleston, won the five-hundred-dollar prize and the commission, though in the interest of holding down costs, Washington suggested that he scale down the design to omit a third story.

John Adams, the first occupant, arrived in 1800 when the plaster was still wet and there were ladders instead of stairs. Adams set a precedent by holding public receptions once a week, but his successor, Thomas Jefferson, went even further, opening the house to the public at all times. Until the time of Theodore Roosevelt, anyone was welcome to stop in and look around. Up until World War II, in fact, visitors could drive up to the north portico, where a butler with a silver tray would receive calling cards.

Changing times and assassination attempts have put chains and guards around the entrances of the house, but everyone is still welcome to tour. Over a million people do so every year, making this the most visited home in the country. As many as six thousand people line up on an average summer day, waiting patiently in line while a voice on a loudspeaker tells them about the history of the house. Often the voice belongs to the resident first lady.

No one emerges without sharing pride in the nation's lovely first residence.

A Grand Tour

While kings and prime ministers enter through the north porte cochere, most tourists today come in through the east wing lobby, which was added in 1942.

Above: *a chandelier and a gilt mirror are repeated endlessly in a matching mirror in the White House's East Room.*

Right: *the President's Oval Office. Though each President subtly varies this room's decor, the flags always remain here.*

Below: *the President's helicopter prepares to land on the White House lawn, where the Press awaits the premier.*

The White House tour includes its most famous first-floor rooms. These are the four state reception rooms – the East, Green, Blue, and Red Rooms – the State Dining Room, and the entrance hall. A VIP tour adds ground floor rooms including the Library, the Vermeil Room, China Room, and the Diplomatic Reception Room. The family dining room and nine rooms upstairs are private.

No room is more memorable than Hoban's oval Blue Room. It was redone in 1972 in regal French Empire style, the decor chosen by President James Monroe in 1817. A settee and seven of the original gilded chairs made for Monroe by Parisian cabinet maker Pierre-Antoine Bellange are the most important pieces of furniture. The walls are covered with a silk-screen reproduction of a French Directoire paper made about 1800, with friezes at top and bottom. The draperies, copied from an early nineteenth-century French design, are blue satin with handmade fringe and gold satin valences. A gilded wood chandelier, white Carrara marble mantel, imperial eagles, urns, and classical figures are all part of the decor, along with an oval rug woven in Peking around 1850.

The Red Room is also furnished in the Empire style of 1810-30. President and Mrs. Lincoln liked this room and used it frequently for informal entertaining. Notable art works in this room are Gilbert Stuart's portrait of Dolley Madison and Albert Bierstadt's *View of the Rocky Mountains*, the latter acquired by President Ronald Reagan.

The Green Room, Federal in style, has served as dining room, sitting room, card room, and lodging room over its long history. Redone in 1972, the walls are covered with the same delicate green watered silk chosen by Jacqueline Kennedy in 1962. The draperies of beige, green, and coral satin stripes are from a nineteenth-century pattern. The French chandelier of cut glass and ormolu is from the nineteenth century.

The East Room was designed by Hoban as a Public Audience Room, and is often used for large gatherings such as dances, concerts, and award ceremonies. Classical in design, it usually contains little furniture other than a Steinway grand piano with gilt American eagle supports and gilt stenciling, given by the manufacturer in 1938. The full length portrait of George Washington on the wall, saved by Dolley Madison from an 1814 fire, is the only object known to have remained in the White House since 1800.

The State Dining Room, resplendent in white and gold, can seat 140. The burnished mahogany table is surrounded by tall Queen Anne-style chairs. It displays some of the gilt service purchased by James Monroe in France in 1817. The ornamental bronze-dore pieces include a centerpiece with seven mirrored sections measuring thirteen feet, six inches.

On the ground floor, the Diplomatic Reception

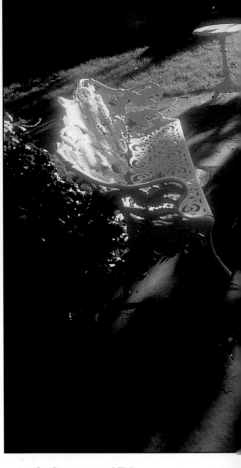

Above: *rich red tulips surround a White House fountain.*

Room, once used as a boiler room, is now furnished as a nineteenth-century drawing room with Sheraton- and Hepplewhite-style furnishings. The striking panoramic wallpaper, "Scenic America," was based on engravings of American landscapes from the 1820s.

Another Gilbert Stuart portrait of George Washington hangs above the fireplace in the Library, which is decorated as a "painted" room typical of the early 1800s. The soft gray paneling dates from a renovation in Harry Truman's term, 1948-52, when old timber removed when the mansion was renovated was reused as paneling for various ground-floor rooms.

Two rooms noted for their collections are the Vermeil Room, exhibiting the collection of vermeil or gilded silver given to the White House by Margaret Thompson Biddle in 1956, and the China Room, designated by Mrs. Woodrow Wilson in 1917 to display the dinnerware used by the various White House occupants.

The ground floor corridor and the rooms opening off it originally were used as a work area. When Abraham Lincoln arrived in 1861, an aide recalled, the basement had "the air of an old unsuccessful hotel." The "fine groined arches" of the original architect, James Hoban, had been cut in all directions to hold pipes. As the result of renovations in 1902 and remodeling during the Truman administration, the elegant vaulted ceiling has been restored and the hall transformed by walls and floors of marble, antique furniture, and works of art.

The custom of hanging portraits of first ladies in this area dates from 1902 when Mrs. Theodore Roosevelt wrote to architect McKim to ask that "all the ladies of the White House, including myself" be removed to the downstairs corridor. Traditionally, portraits of recent first ladies are hung outside the entry to the Diplomatic Reception Room.

History of the House

The present decor of the White House is as it might have been done in the first third of the nineteenth century if our forefathers had had all the taste and money they needed. That, however, was not the case.

Like its home town, the White House took a long time to reach its present elegant state. Many times the furnishings were allowed to become shabby and the house itself to slip into serious decay.

At the beginning, it was a struggle just to get the building constructed on time. President John Adams found shelter when he arrived, but few comforts. His wife, Abigail, wrote to her daughter about some of her problems, cautioning her to keep the complaints secret. "Not one room or chamber of the work is finished . . . we have not the least fence, yard or other convenience without, and the great unfinished audience room I make a drying room of, to hang the clothes in." New Englanders, commented Mrs. Adams, would have done a better job of finishing things.

Records show that one James Clark was hired with orders to get the back stairs and a privy built within a fortnight, then to complete the interior doors and

Left: *garden chairs – typical White House informality.*

Above: *the lantern over the White House carriage entrance.*

grand window at the east end of the house. Apparently when the first lady had laundry hung up to dry in the East Room, it flapped in winter winds.

Thomas Jefferson, the first president to spend a full term in the house, began efforts to improve things and to furnish the residence in style. His efforts were halted in 1803 when Benjamin Latrobe, surveyor of the public buildings, looked things over and ordered a new roof. So much rainwater had leaked through the ceiling of the East Room that the ceiling had collapsed and the back walls had started to spread. Latrobe shored things up with sheet iron, but this was the first of several occasions when the White House suffered dangerous deterioration.

It was Jefferson himself who designed the low-lying east and west pavilions for household and official work. Latrobe completed them in 1807 and built a fireproof vault for the treasury at the far end of the east colonnade. Hoban also designed a semi-circular portico for the south front and a larger one with a "porte cochere" or carriage port for the north. Jefferson approved the plans, but the south entrance was not actually completed until 1924, the north until 1929.

Jefferson introduced an informal lifestyle to the President's House, sometimes coming to the door in his slippers. But furnishings were another matter. Here, his tastes were sumptuous. He was particularly fond of the style known as Louis XVI in France and Federal in America.

When James Madison arrived in 1809, his wife Dolley decorated in a style that was described as "immense and magnificent." The glory did not last, however. The British set fire to the building during the war of 1812. When she fled, Mrs. Madison managed to take with her a carriage load of cabinet papers in trunks, as well as the government's silver, and she broke an ornate frame to rescue Gilbert Stuart's canvas of George Washington, now one of the chief White House treasures.

James Hoban, the original architect, took charge of rebuilding the mansion, and when it was habitable again in 1817, Congress appropriated twenty thousand dollars for furnishings. James Monroe, who had acquired fine Louis XVI furnishings of his own as a diplomat in Paris, sold these to the government and ordered an array of goods from France and from American cabinetmakers to supplement it. When crowds arrived on January 1, 1818, to see the President's House in its new splendor, they found the Oval Room aglow with gilded Empire furniture from Bellange of Paris, fine silks, ornaments of porcelain, silver, and bronze, and a fifty-candle chandelier. Items remaining or repurchased from the Monroe restoration are the heart of the historic collection of the White House.

Through the rest of the nineteenth century, most of the occupants of the White House preferred furnishings in the contemporary fashion of the day, selling inherited pieces at public auction as they

27

Above: *the bronze* Statue of Freedom *that surmounts the Capitol dome. It is nineteen-and-a-half-feet high.*

Left: *sunset tinges the Capitol with softest pink. Night and day, political issues remain the capital's lifeblood.*

Right: *the nine-million-pound, cast-iron dome of the Capitol, designed and painted to resemble marble.*

became worn. This did not take long. Furnishings in a much-used public building take hard wear, and by 1825, an inventory already showed that fabrics and many of the purchases made by the Madisons had become "altogether useless."

There were regular appropriations to keep up the house, but a president out of favor with Congress could expect arguments over his household budgets. John Adams had trouble when he was accused of buying horses with money earmarked for furniture, and his son had similar problems over the purchase of a billiard table when he took office in 1824.

Though he came into office as a frontiersman, Andrew Jackson was all elegance when he took over the White House. He revived the long-deferred plan for the North Portico, and was the first to properly furnish the East Room. A great entertainer, Jackson bought rich new tumblers and wine glasses and

French porcelain dinnerware. He also installed plumbing for running water.

His successor, Martin Van Buren, had the bad luck to come in during a depression. He was portrayed as a sissified spendthrift, and he lost the next election. When William Henry Harrison died within a month of taking office, John Tyler was left with the burden of raising funds for the White House. He was refused and the furnishings deteriorated badly. Upholstered only once since 1817, the chairs reached a condition described as "perfect explosion at every prominent point that presents contact with the outer garments of the visitors." Those in the East Room, one journal wrote, would disgrace a house of shame.

Money became available again for James Polk in 1845, and an era of Victorian fancy took over the White House. Modern amenities such as an ice box and gas lights were installed in 1849.

Heating remained a problem, though Hoban had added twelve fireplaces when he rebuilt the structure in 1817, and Martin Van Buren had added a furnace. Franklin Pierce was the president who can be credited with adding an improved heating plant – as well as a new bathroom.

Every president left his mark on the White House, but some more than others. James Buchanan, a dignified bachelor, was known for gracious entertaining. He began the presidential portrait collection with an allotment of five thousand dollars to buy portraits of five former presidents. He also gained twenty thousand dollars for a new conservatory and remodeled the Blue Room, where Monroe's furniture had stood since 1817. It was replaced with a rococo-revival suite that served for decades. Except for the one large pier table, Monroe's beautiful Bellange pieces were sold at auction.

By the time the Lincolns moved in, Washington was a war town. Guards patrolled the porticoes with muskets and slept in the East Room. Yet Mary Lincoln was determined to make it into a home, and she overran the appropriation given them by sixty-seven hundred dollars. The angry president refused to submit the bill to Congress.

Andrew Johnson's difficulties with Congress did not include appropriations for the White House. The Blue Room was re-decorated by his daughter, Martha Patterson, in 1867. Ulysses S. Grant continued the renovation in 1873, at the height of the gilded age. By this time the house was showing its years seriously. A report from the commissioner of public buildings noted that a large ceiling had collapsed, that all were cracked, and that the basement was damp and unhealthy. He also mentioned that closets were now considered indispensable and that the White House had none. The commissioner added, "it hardly seems possible to state anything in favor of the house as a

Above: *the central portion of the West Front of the Capitol, designed by Charles Bulfinch.*

Left: *the Capitol's dome, which echoes St. Peter's in Rome and St. Paul's in London.*

Right: *the "Landmark of Liberty" dominates the Washington skyline.*

residence; but if thoroughly repaired, it would serve its purpose admirably as an executive office."

National sentiment, however, decreed that the White House retain its place as the chief executive's home, even though the size of the office staff was rapidly multiplying, swelled by the massive job of reconstruction following the Civil War.

In the years 1882-84, Chester A. Arthur swept out furniture by the wagonload. A "decayed furnishings" auction brought out five thousand bidders for the marble mantles, cuspidors, hair mattresses, and curtains put up for sale. Arthur also made needed repairs to modernize the mansion and hired Louis C. Tiffany to redecorate the state rooms. When Cleveland married in 1886 (the first president to wed in office), his new wife instituted Saturday afternoon "levees," inviting working women in to meet the lady of the White House. (The term "first lady" did not come into use until 1900).

Next came Benjamin Harrison, with an entourage that strained the five-bedroom White House. It included his wife, her ninety-year-old father, their son Russell

and his wife and daughter, their daughter, Mary Mckee, with two small children, and his wife's sister and niece. Understandably, Mrs. Harrison began a campaign for enlarging and improving the White House. She left a lasting mark. Her investigation of an old china closet led to the beginning of the White House china collection, which now represents almost every president through Ronald Reagan. Her interest in history prompted the establishment of an historical art wing.

Harrison's favorite part of the renovation was the new white tile and marble bathroom, complete with porcelain lined tub. "They would tempt a duck to wash himself every day," he said.

Back to the Beginning

As Washington's centennial celebration as capital city approached, there were dreams of restoring the city to meet L'Enfants original vision. Architect Glenn Brown was supported in his suggestion that the White House should be enlarged and restored to this ideal,

though there were still those who were convinced that the President needed a new home.

When McKinley's assassination brought Theodore Roosevelt to the White House in 1901, he dismissed any notion of living elsewhere. Instead, he called in the noted firm of McKim, Mead & White to design new offices and redo the state rooms. Once again, the architects declared the house in need of immediate repair. The ground floor was in bad condition and most of the state floor was settling dangerously. The flooring on the second level needed total replacement, and the wiring and insulation were worn. The entire interior was reconstructed and a new basement dug for the heating system.

This was the renovation that restored Jefferson's west pavilion to lead to new executive offices and rebuilt the east pavilion to shelter arriving visitors. It also provided cloakroom space, needed since the days when Andrew Jackson's admirers hung their coats on the fence outside.

McKim's classical taste and painstaking decoration

obliterated the excesses of the Victorians and returned the house to its original design. There have been alterations and modernizations since that time, but maintaining the authentic look of early years has remained a primary goal ever since.

With the stress of constantly growing numbers of visitors, it was hoped that the American people would pitch in to support giving the White House the elegance it deserved. Grace Coolidge lobbied Congress to authorize the acceptance of appropriate antiques as gifts. A group was appointed to evaluate donations. Herbert Hoover recalled from storage four of Lincoln's cabinet chairs and grouped them with other furniture of the Lincoln-Grant era in his second-floor study. Mrs. Hoover catalogued furnishings and commissioned copies of the furniture used by James Monroe.

As the country went through a depression and a world war, little attention was paid to decor during Franklin Roosevelt's long term of office. His successor, Harry Truman, had hardly finished adding a controversial balcony when once again there were dire

31

reports that the building showed signs of collapsing. The Trumans moved to Blair House while twenty-seven months of work began. This last major renovation added new underpinnings, a two-story basement and foundations, and a steel frame. the interior was restored with fidelity except for the main stairway, which was changed to descend dramatically into the entrance hall.

Truman hoped to furnish the restored White House with antiques and important artifacts from the past, but once again it was a case of stormy relations with Congress and an inadequate budget. He did receive some antiques as gifts after a TV appeal. Later, Jacqueline Kennedy guided fellow citizens through the White House room by room on a television tour, stirring public interest. In 1961, Mrs. Kennedy formed a Fine Arts Committee for the White House in order to acquire appropriate items, with guidance from museum experts and a curatorial staff. A special committee on paintings soon followed. The Eighty-seventh Congress provided that furniture of historic or artistic interest might become inalienable property of the White House and that the ground floor corridor and principal public rooms of the first floor would be recognized as of "museum character."

In 1965, President Lyndon Johnson carried on the campaign by establishing the Committee for the Preservation of the White House, staffed with a permanent curator. During the Nixon years, valuable pieces of furniture and American paintings were acquired, including portraits from life of several presidents and first ladies.

Patricia Nixon began another major program of needed renovation in 1969, and the next five years saw all the principal rooms on the state and ground floors redecorated. Rosalyn Carter helped add another thirty-four American paintings to the collections, while President Jimmy Carter showed particular interest in furnishings associated with former White House inhabitants. Interest spurred by Nancy Reagan brought redecoration of the second- and third-floor rooms as well as special preservation projects for rooms on the state floor. Many fine pieces of early nineteenth-century American furniture already in the collection were taken from storage, refinished, and returned to service.

The effort to make the White House's formal rooms a showcase for the nation continues. After all, as an anonymous writer said back in 1834, "This is the only *PALACE* in the United States."

The East Portico of the Capitol, where the President is inaugurated.

The Capitol

The *Statue of Freedom* stands tall atop the United States Capitol building. On her base, the words "E Pluribus Unum" – out of many, one.

Thomas Jefferson called the Capitol, "the first temple dedicated to the sovereignty of the people," and for almost two hundred years, representatives of the county's divergent voices have, indeed, come together here, forging the laws of the land. One hundred senators and 435 representatives from every part of the country convene to guard the sometimes conflicting interests of their constituents. Somehow they manage to negotiate compromise through negotiation and debate. If not perfect, Congress remains a shining example of democracy in action.

The structure itself is Washington's most imposing building. A city ordinance limiting buildings to thirteen stories insures that it will remain the town's tallest structure.

The most striking features are the splendid dome and the columned porticoes that adorn the building on all sides, with magnificent flights of steps leading up to them. The grand east front is where most presidents have taken the oath of office. The west front also sparkles in the sun, fresh from a recent restoration. In 1981, Ronald Reagan broke with tradition and held his inaugural here.

The Capitol is the heart of the U.S. government, and most Americans as well as foreign visitors want to see it for themselves. A staff of more than thirty guides lead tours that leave every three to five minutes. An average of one hundred and ninety-two thousand visitors come on a busy day in April, a popular month for families taking advantage of Easter school break. The tour leads through the Rotunda, the Statuary Hall, the old Supreme Court, and old Senate Chambers. There is a stop in the gallery to watch the legislators in action, but many a visitor is puzzled to see that there is very little going on most of the time, perhaps a lone speaker addressing a nearly empty row of seats. Most of the real work in Congress is done in committees and behind the scenes. Most committee meetings are also open to the public. Congressional "action" on the floor of the House or Senate is seen best when a big controversial vote is scheduled, with heated oratory and everyone rushing in to be counted.

An interesting historical note: with one exception, the desks in the Senate are the same ones that were installed when each state was admitted to the Union. Daniel Webster, the senator from New Hampshire, was not happy when writing boxes were added to the desks in the 1850s and turned his down. His successor asked that the original desk be given to that state, and it was done.

Left: *the classical pediment of the House of Representatives, the south wing of the Capitol, added in 1916.*

Facing page top: *the bronze statue that surmounts the Capitol dome, planned as* Armed Liberty *by its sculptor.*

Facing page bottom: *Washington basks in the warmth of a spring morning as mist from the Potomac clears.*

Capitol History

When the American Revolution ended, the new United States was in immediate need of a building to house its Congress. It was not surprising that the inspiration came from the great architecture of Europe. William Thornton, Benjamin Latrobe, and Charles Bulfinch were the creators of the "Old Capitol" completed in 1826. Thomas U. Walter designed the major extensions begun in 1851.

The area selected for "the Congress House" by L'Enfant was Jenkins Hill, a plateau eighty-eight feet above the level of the Potomac River. He called it "a pedestal awaiting a monument." Advertisements were

placed offering a prize of five hundred pounds for the "most approved plan." None of the sixteen plans submitted pleased the judges. Dr. William Thornton, a physician and self-taught architect of Tortola, West Indies, was granted permission to submit a plan after the deadline, and it was Thornton's design that was selected. The cornerstone was laid by George

Washington on September 18, 1793, with full Masonic honors. According to reports, he was wearing an apron embroidered for him by Lafayette's wife.

Thornton's plan followed the Palladian concept. The rotunda and dome were reminiscent of the Pantheon in Rome. North and south rectangular wings flanked either side. Classic Corinthian columns and capitals were used.

The northern wing was the first to be completed in 1800, and in this small building were housed a legislature of 32 senators and 106 congressmen, the Supreme Court, circuit courts, and the Library of Congress. Thomas Jefferson was inaugurated in this cramped Senate chamber in 1801. In 1803, Jefferson appointed Benjamin Latrobe as surveyor of public buildings. Under his supervision, the House of Representatives wing was finished and connected to the north wing by a wooden walkway. The House moved into its chamber in the south wing in 1807, though it was not totally completed until 1811. There were almost immediate complaints of the roof leaking and plaster falling.

Above: *the blending of marble and white-painted cast iron that makes the Capitol so impressive a building.*

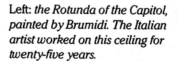

Left: *the Rotunda of the Capitol, painted by Brumidi. The Italian artist worked on this ceiling for twenty-five years.*

Overseeing repairs in the Senate wing, Latrobe installed six columns to support the weight of the vaulted ceiling, relieving the walls. In designing these columns, he deserted two thousand years of Greco–Roman tradition and decorated the capitals with carved corn cobs and tobacco leaves, symbols of the New World's agriculture.

Like most of Washington, the Capitol building was burned by the British on August 14, 1814. Latrobe took charge of the rebuilding. In the Senate chamber, he also added more support columns, twelve caryatids in the form of draped female figures, bringing the complete number of columns to twenty, one for each state. The story goes that he asked for Italian marble rather than the Virginia freestone originally used. When Congress refused to be so extravagant, Latrobe resigned.

He was replaced in 1819 by Charles Bulfinch, the first American-born head of the construction, who was responsible for the center section and low wooden dome of the Capitol. It was larger than either Thornton or Latrobe had envisioned. The "Bulfinch" dome of wood covered with copper was the dominant feature of the building for more than a quarter of a century. His great Rotunda was an important element of the building. Completed in 1824, the Rotunda became the reception room for official visits and the place where the nation pays final tribute to its most

The view from the top of the Rotunda. Brumidi's trompe l'oeil frieze, painted to look like sculpture, depicts events in the nation's history, starting with Columbus' landing in the New World.

eminent citizens by having their remains lie in state before burial.

Among the most moving moments in the Rotunda was the tribute to John Fitzgerald Kennedy on November 24 and 25, 1963, following the young president's assassination. Perhaps the most unusual occasion came in 1919 when Major Pierre Charles L'Enfant, Washington's original architect, was belatedly honored on the occasion of his re-internment at Arlington Cemetery.

The Walter Era

After Bulfinch completed his work in 1829, there was no official architect of the Capitol again until 1851, when expanding needs of Congress made additions necessary. A competition was held once again, and the plans submitted by Thomas U. Walter, a noted Philadelphia architect, were selected. Walter became official architect of the Capitol until 1865, directing the expansion of the House and Senate wings. The present House chamber was occupied on December 16, 1857, and the Senate met for the first time in its present chamber on January 4, 1859.

The move for the Senate meant leaving quarters

Left: *the Capitol's bronze Statue of Freedom whose headdress has led many to believe she is an Indian.*

Facing page top: *the photographer's zoom lens draws light from the Capitol, the hub of Washington.*

Facing page bottom: *the Stars and Stripes on the Capitol billow out against a Washington summer sky.*

The acoustics in the old chamber were unusual. John Quincy Adams was said to have found a certain spot where he could hear every whisper on the floor. In a quirk of fate, when he returned as a legislator after his term as president, he collapsed from a stroke on that very spot. He was carried out and died in an adjacent room.

The Dome and the "Statue of Freedom"

The additions to the Capitol made a new dome desirable to preserve the good proportions of the building. Beginning in 1856, the Bulfinch dome was replaced with a much higher design by Walter. Recognizing that halting the project would hurt morale, Abraham Lincoln had the work continue in the midst of the Civil War. The new tiered dome was lifted into place in December 1863. The iron dome weighed in at some 8,909,200 pounds.

The crowning touch was the bronze statue atop the dome. Officially known as the *Statue of Freedom*, the statue stands nineteen feet, six inches tall. It was designed by American sculptor Thomas Crawford, who was also responsible for the bronze doors of the House and Senate wings. He received three thousand dollars for the plaster model, which was executed in his studio in Rome. Crawford died in 1857, never to see his statue in place.

Beneath the dome in the rotunda, 180 feet from the floor, Italian immigrant Constantino Brumidi was

where much history had been made. It had only recently been the scene of historic debates with great orators Henry Clay, Daniel Webster, and John C. Calhoun arguing the issues of slavery and states' rights. So heated were feelings on both sides that in 1857 Representative Preston Brooks of South Carolina attacked Senator Sumner of Massachusetts with a cane.

When it was no longer needed, Congress decided to use the semi-circular marble Senate chamber as a Statuary Hall. In 1864, each state was invited to send two statues of notable citizens for display. In the 1930s, due to fear that the weight would cause the marble floor to collapse, some of the statues were moved to other parts of the building.

The old House had its own historic yarns to tell.

commissioned to paint a fresco, the *Apotheosis of Washington*, with figures twenty-five feet high. The project took him twenty-five years.

The finished Capitol building had impressive statistics – a floor area of 16½ acres and some 540 rooms.

The Modern Capitol

It was almost a century before further major alterations were made to the Capitol – between 1949 and 1951. At that time, roofs and skylights were replaced with new roofs of concrete and steel, covered with copper. Air conditioning, lighting, and acoustics also were improved.

In 1956, further reconstruction and needed replacement of the central portion of the Capitol was authorized by Congress. From 1958 to 1962, a new east front in marble was constructed, faithfully reproducing the design of the old sandstone front, but placed 32½ feet east of the original front. The old sandstone walls remained in place, becoming part of the interior wall.

The west-front renovation was completed in 1987. Here preservationists won out over expansionists and the original facade remained in place.

Frederick Law Olmsted's design for the grounds of

Above: the light blue roofs of Washington's government buildings.

Facing page: frescoes in the Senate Reception Room of the Capitol.

Below: yachting on the Potomac River in the heart of the capital.

the building included terraces on the north, west, and south sides of the Capitol. These were constructed between 1884 and 1892, then further enlarged and improved by the annexation and development of 61.4 acres of land north of Constitution Avenue during the

Court House subway station. Washington can boast one of the most modern subways in the country, which succeeds in making cross-town travel considerably quicker than it could be by road.

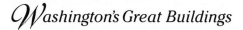

period 1910-35. The grounds continued to be gradually increased and improved. The original Olmsted terraces were restored in 1987.

The Capitol Subway System

One of the most intriguing additions to the Capitol was a pedestrian tunnel connecting the Capitol with the office buildings for members of the Senate. As soon as the tunnel was completed in 1908, things were speeded up by the addition of a vehicle. The first four-wheeled, eight passenger coaches with solid rubber tires were delivered in 1909, but by 1912, a faster and safer electric monorail system was developed, upping capacity to eighteen passengers. That was replaced in 1960 by a system using two cars shuttling back and forth with a one-way running time of forty-five seconds. A second line now also makes the run in sixty seconds to the Dirksen Office Building used by House of Representatives members. The speed is greatly appreciated when congressmen hurry

Tulips are an annual arrival in the Capitol area, where the parkland is much the same today as it was when the landscape artist Frederick Law Olmstead laid it out at the turn of the century.

to the floor to be counted for a vote.

One of the original cars, still a sentimental favorite, is displayed in the Senate's Russell Office Building rotunda; the second car was given to the Smithsonian Institution.

The Supreme Court

While Congress enacts the nation's laws, it is the Supreme Court that is the final word on defining that law and deciding controversial issues. This makes it the most powerful judicial body in the world. Yet the Court did not have a building to call its own until 1935. Up to that time, it was quartered in the Capitol building.

When it was finally built, the Court was provided with a Neo-Classic building of white Vermont marble

situated close to the Capitol. Designed by Cass Gilbert, the edifice is reminiscent of a Greek temple and is both dignified and commanding. The sculpture on the pediment requires a closer look, since the faces of the statues are recognizable people. As well as those of former Chief Justices, Gilbert included his own portrait and those of some of his non-judicial associates in the group depicted. Together they represent the concerns of the court: Liberty, Authority, Order and Research.

Two massive bronze doors lead into an ornate entrance hall with a coffered ceiling and marble columns, a scene made even grander by the subdued light. Inside are two grand spaces, the Great Hall and the Court Room, each with classical colonnades. Busts of all the former Chief Justices are found inside the Great Hall.

Left: *one of two marble figures of Justice that are seated either side of the steps of the Supreme Court Building, close to the Capitol. Here the nation's foremost judges decide on crucial points of law.*

Below: *the imposing facade of the Federal Reserve, nicknamed the "Temple of the Dollar." Built in 1937, the building has an Art Deco feel. Here, high-finance meetings may be attended by the public.*

Right: *the Treasury Building, the oldest departmental office in the city. Its construction took thirty-three years.*

The Court is in session from the first Monday in October to the end of April. Oral arguments are heard for two weeks of the month, usually from 10 a.m. to noon and 1 p.m. to 3 p.m. Monday to Wednesday. Each of the 150 cases heard is allotted one hour, 30 minutes for each side. Some decisions are announced before hearings. More are made after the session is over, in May and June, with the most important coming usually near the end of the term, around the Fourth of July.

The public is welcome to listen in on both arguments and decisions, and this is one branch of government where the leading figures are always in attendance. Often the attorneys' presentations and the probing questions from the justices are fascinating. The gallery seats two hundred people, and when the case is controversial, lines are long. Visitors are also invited to an exhibit depicting major events in Court history, a movie about the Supreme Court, and a talk by a member of the curatorial staff.

Right: *visitors pose for a photograph on the pristine limestone steps of Washington National Cathedral.*

Washington National Cathedral, begun in 1907 when Teddy Roosevelt officiated at the ground-breaking ceremony.

The National Cathedral, the sixth largest in the world. Designed in the Gothic style of the fourteenth century, the cathedral was completed in 1990. It does not have its own congregation and opens its doors to worshippers of all denominations.

Left: *choir boys pause on the marble aisle of a deserted National Cathedral on their way to choir practice. The cathedral is the seat of the Washington Episcopal diocese.*

Above: *the exterior stone carving of the magnificent West Rose Window of Washington National Cathedral.*

Left: *sunlight through the National Cathedral's stained glass turns its Gothic-style statues to purple and gold. Such statues are proof that medieval skills of stonemasonry have survived intact.*

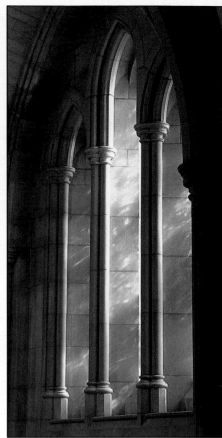

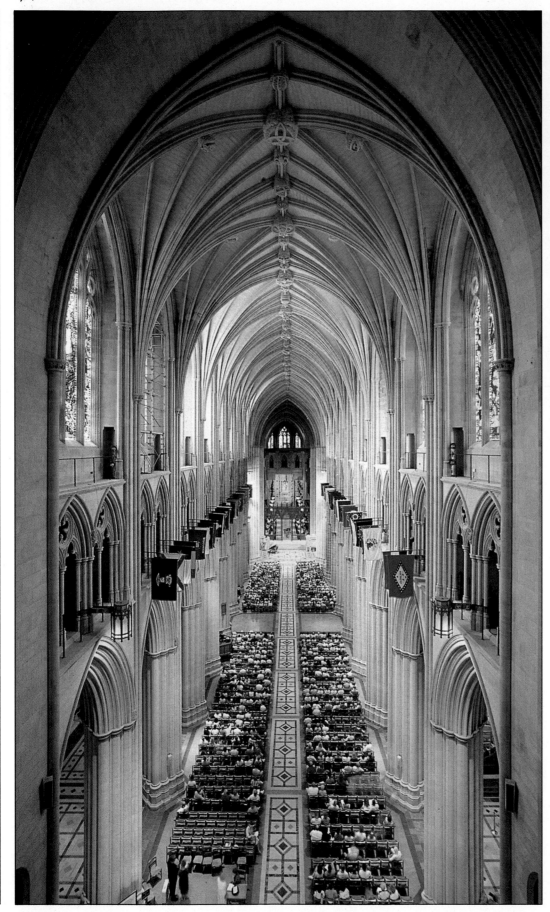

Above: *invisible yet evident – stained glass in Washington Cathedral. The nave houses scores of stained-glass windows.*

Left: *the majestic nave of Washington National Cathedral, lined with flags and tiled in colored marble.*

Facing page: *the National Cathedral in midwinter. Set high on Mount Saint Alban Hill, it can be seen all over the city.*

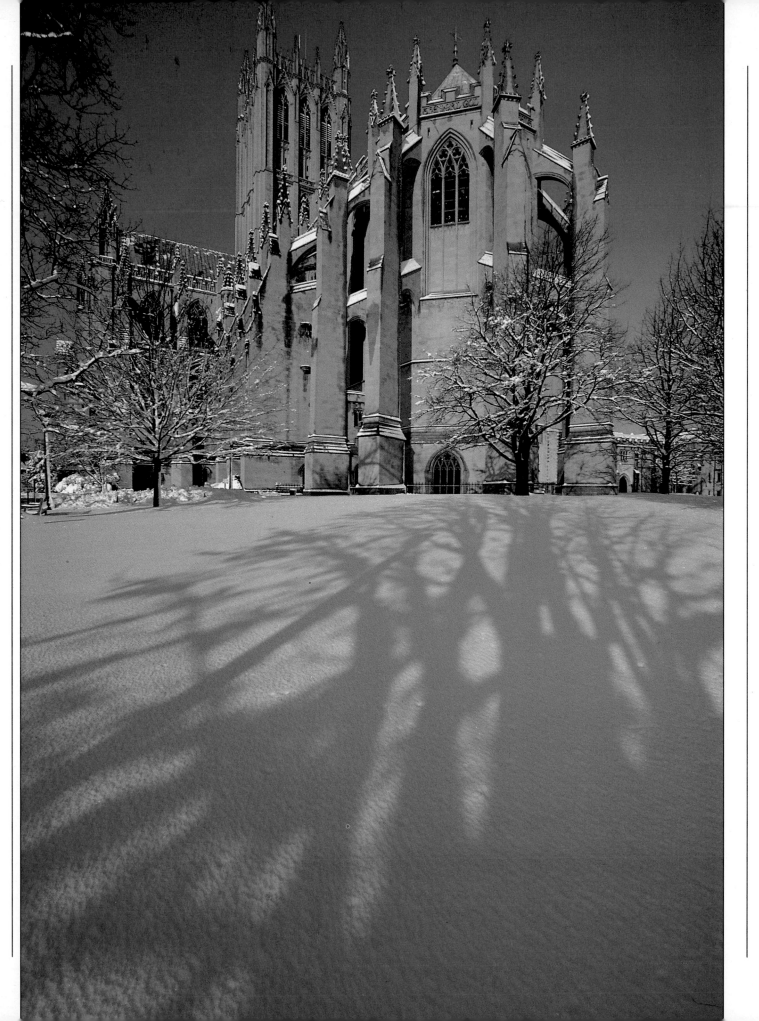

Left: *a golden angel Moroni raises a trumpet atop one of the six spires of the Latter Day Saints Temple in Maryland.*

Above: *the Netherlands Carrillon, Arlington Cemetery, a gift to the American people from the Dutch.*

Below: *the Latter Day Saints Temple, Kennington, opened in 1974. Entry is for Mormons only.*

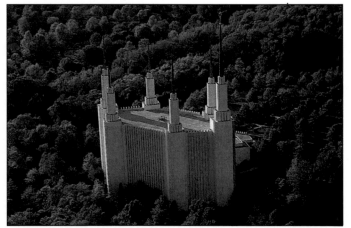

Above: *the Islamic Center, a cultural and religious center maintained by the Islamic embassies based in the capital.*

Right: *the National Shrine of the Immaculate Conception, the largest Catholic church in the Western hemisphere.*

Below: *a statue of St. Francis of Assisi in the Franciscan Monastery.*

Left: *a swathe of mist gives the Xerox Training Center a mysterious, almost science fictional appearance.*

Above: *the enclosed courtyard of the National Building Museum, formerly the old Pension Building.*

Left: *the headquarters of the Organization of American States, one of the capital's most striking buildings.*

Above: *the Criminal Investigation Agency Building. From here the C.I.A. organizes its work around the world.*

Facing page: *the beige concrete Federal Bureau of Investigation Building looms over a passerby on Pennsylvania Avenue.*

Right: *the sober facade of the American Pharmaceutical Association Building, which lies near the Lincoln Memorial.*

Left: *a couple stroll down a modern cloister in Georgetown University, the first Roman Catholic college in the U.S.A.*

An aerial view of Georgetown University, which was established in 1789. Although a Catholic university, from its inception Georgetown has been open to students of every religious profession and now includes people from ninety-one countries.

Above: *sunset, Georgetown, the spire of the Healy Building lending a romantic air to this view across the Potomac.*

Left: *blossom on an old cherry tree brightens the grounds of Georgetown University on a grey spring afternoon.*

Facing page: *a dusting of snow on the trees beside the Potomac River emphasizes the dark bulk of Georgetown University.*

Above: *the campus of Gallaudet College, the only higher education institute for deaf mutes in existence.*

Facing page: *Howard Hall, Howard University, first used in 1867. This is the oldest black university in the U.S.A.*

Right: *Gallaudet College, named for Thomas Hopkins Gallaudet, who founded the college in 1866.*

Above: *the Washington Monument soars to 555 feet.*
Right: *flags representing the fifty states encircle the Monument, symbolizing the nation's commitment to Washington's ideals.*

The Memorials

The Grand Avenue that L'Enfant planned from the Capitol to the White House and beyond, now known as the Mall, was slow to be realized. For years it was a neglected marshland, so swampy in places that the Washington Monument could not safely be built on its intended spot. When the Lincoln Memorial was proposed, the speaker of the House supposedly grumbled that it would be in the middle of a "damned swamp." Alexander Shepherd, who cleaned up much of the city in the early 1870s, somehow neglected the Mall, even allowing railroad tracks and a depot to be built on it. The unfinished Washington Monument was a further embarrassment. It was not until the beginning of the twentieth century that the MacMillan Commission undertook the draining and landscaping that would at last create the beautiful green that is now a showplace for monuments, museums, and memorials. Washington's most important memorials are here.

The Washington Monument

A memorial to George Washington was ordered by the Continental Congress in 1783, long before there was a permanent capital city. It was to be an equestrian statue of General Washington to stand wherever the headquarters of the Congress would be established.

Unfortunately, Congress failed to supply the money to carry out this plan. A century passed between the act and the actual memorial, and the general on horseback became a towering obelisk that now stands on the Mall, a memorial not only to the first president but to the nation's beginnings. In its very simplicity, it remains one of the most beautiful and memorable of Washington's monuments.

Above: *the Washington Monument in spring.*

Above: *a couple brave the cold to stroll on a windy winter's afternoon to the foot of the Washington Monument.*

Facing page: *rockets shoot even higher than Washington's highest structure during the capital's July 4 celebrations.*

Left: *like surreal flowers, July 4 fireworks spangle the Monument, their transience emphasizing its solidity.*

When Congress finally got around to commissioning Horatio Grenough to create a Washington statue, which was unveiled in the Capitol rotunda in 1841, there was only controversy. Washington was depicted like a Roman emperor, semi-nude in classical costume, his right hand pointing skyward, his left holding a sword.

This was definitely not the memorial the nation wanted for its great leader. Many thought it a scandal to show the general in this kind of scanty costume. It was moved outside the grounds in 1843, and eventually given to the Smithsonian. It is presently on display in the National Museum of American History.

Local citizens, including Chief Justice John Marshall, formed a Washington National Monument Society, hoping to raise money by public subscription for a fitting memorial. The group solicited proposals, and the winner was the obelisk design by noted architect Robert Mills. Mills altered the traditional proportions of obelisks to create a form of special grace and delicacy.

His total design was ambitious. In addition to an obelisk rising nearly six hundred feet, he wanted a Pantheon-like base one hundred feet high to house statues of the nation's founders and patriots. Lack of funds vetoed the elaborate base, and the simple splendid unadorned shaft was begun. The cornerstone was laid with elaborate ceremony on July 4, 1848, using a trowel Washington had used at the laying of the cornerstone of the Capitol in 1793.

Above: *the Washington Monument rises out of a foaming sea of cherry blossom to pierce a cloudless blue sky.*

Left: *double exposure centers the Monument amid a swirl of clouds, its ring of flags appearing to bow before it.*

Right: *a symbol of the capital. It is possible to ascend the obelisk and view the city and Virginia and Maryland beyond.*

But times were not the best for fund-raising. Political quarrels and the growing antagonism between North and South meant that collections lagged, and construction was "temporarily" suspended in 1854. For more than 20 years, the shaft stood unfinished at about 150 feet.

Work was begun again by the Army Corps of Engineers in 1876, this time with a congressional appropriation of two hundred thousand dollars. A slight change in stone color marks the line where construction was resumed. It was discovered that the shaft had tilted because the original foundation was unsound, so a new thirteen-foot-thick concrete foundation was laid. The capstone was set in place on December 6, 1884.

The 555-foot obelisk is still the tallest masonry structure in the world and the most prominent feature of Washington's landscape, usually the first landmark spied by visitors arriving by air. The top presents an inspiring view. It can be reached by a climb of exactly 897 steps, but only the determined need worry about the stairs. The present elevator, installed in 1959, makes the ascent in a swift seventy seconds. Some 188 tribute blocks in the interior walls were sent by states, nations, towns, and other organizations wishing to honor George Washington.

Left: *the tallest masonry structure in the world, which received its aluminum capstone in 1884.*

Below: *a stiff breeze off the Potomac River tugs at the flags that surround this simple, unadorned monument.*

Above: *the dome of the Natural History Museum and the flags of the Washington Monument color a winter's afternoon.*

Lincoln Memorial

It seemed obvious to many, after the tragic assassination of President Lincoln in 1865, that the president who had saved the Union deserved a memorial of some kind. A pyramid, or an obelisk, or a memorial avenue were among the suggestions considered then, but Congress could not reach agreement. Only with the hindsight granted them as the years passed by did the matter become easier to decide, and in 1911 the architect Henry Bacon and the sculptor Daniel Chester French were given the task of creating a truly monumental building. In 1922 it was finished, and one of the most impressive memorials in America took its place in Washington.

Henry Bacon had designed a white marble temple surrounded by thirty-six simple columns. Inside, Daniel Chester French housed what many have since considered to be his masterpiece – a giant statue of the president seated squarely on a throne-like chair, his beautifully carved hands resting on the arms, a thoughtful, resolute expression on his face. It is a face familiar to all Americans, since it appears on the U.S. penny.

Carvers worked for four years to fashion the statue, which is made from twenty-eight blocks of Georgia marble. The figure is set on a ten-foot-high base of Tennessee marble. A fitting sentiment is inscribed on the wall behind Lincoln's head: "In this

Above: *the Lincoln Memorial glows at night as if lit by a great inner fire. In appearance, this flat-roofed Greek temple is not dissimilar to the Parthenon. The marble comes from Colorado.*

Right: *Lincoln's statue, the centerpiece of the Lincoln Memorial and one of the most famous sculptures in America. It was dedicated in 1922, fifty-seven years after the death of the "Great Emancipator."*

temple, as in the hearts of the people for whom he saved the Union, the memory of Abraham Lincoln is enshrined forever."

Also engraved in stone on the memorial's north wall is Lincoln's Gettysburg Address. His second inaugural address is on the south wall, accompanied by Jules Guerin's painted murals entitled *Emancipation of a Race* and *Reunion and Progress*.

These titles seemed to set the atmosphere for the memorial, which in recent years has become a rallying point for Civil Rights marchers, though, ironically, the 1922 dedication ceremony was segregated. Twenty years later, as a protest at her treatment by the D.A.R. who had refused to let her sing at Constitution Hall, the black contralto Marian Anderson chose to sing on the steps of the Lincoln Memorial. She had an audience of 75,000 people. In 1968 Martin Luther King, Jr. made his "I Have A Dream" speech from the same steps.

The top of these steps is the perfect place for a reverse view of the Mall, a view as inspiring as the one from the Capitol esplanade. The reflection of the Washington Monument in the long pool separating the two memorials is one of the most photographed in the world.

Above: *the Lincoln Memorial at night, as dramatically lit as a stage set, just as the sculptor, Daniel Chester French, intended.*

Facing page: *a cloud-covered sky heavy with snow forms a midwinter backcloth to the Lincoln Memorial.*

The Lincoln Memorial, which faces the Washington Monument and backs onto the Potomac River.

The Jefferson Memorial. This marble structure rests on steel cylinders filled with concrete driven deep into the bedrock and countersunk in this site of reclaimed landfill.

Jefferson Memorial

The remarkable man who is credited with writing the Declaration of Independence and who served the nation as its third president waited almost 150 years to be accorded his country's ultimate tribute. The Jefferson Memorial was completed in 1942 with the strong backing of President Franklin Delano Roosevelt, in spite of strong opposition from many who objected to the prominent site facing the lovely pond known as the Tidal Basin. Exasperated by conservationists who threatened to chain themselves to the cherry trees to save the trees from being cut down to make room for the building, Roosevelt said, "If the tree is in the way,

Above: *the Greek portico and pediment of the Jefferson Memorial. Its steps afford a good view of the White House.*

The Jefferson Memorial from the air. The third President would have approved of the choice of a rotunda, since it was one of his favorite architectural features, used by him at Monticello.

Above: the statue of Jefferson, unveiled on the bicentennial of his birth in 1943. As there was a wartime ban on domestic metal, a plaster statue instead of a bronze one was displayed then.

Above: the Memorial floodlit at night. The pediment shows Jefferson with the co-authors of the Declaration of Independence.

Facing page: four entrances bring light and air into the graceful chamber of the Memorial, one of the most popular in Washington.

we will move the tree and the lady and the chains and transplant them to some other place."

The soaring white rotunda and white marble columns of the Jefferson Memorial reflect the classical forms of ancient Rome. The rotunda designed by John Russell Pope was a fitting form since Jefferson, who was an accomplished architect, used rotundas at the University of Virginia and at his home, Monticello, his two most famous achievements.

Sculptor Rudolph Evans's nineteen-foot bronze of a standing Jefferson portrays the great man at middle age. The walls of the memorial bear excerpts from the two documents for which Jefferson most wanted to be

81

remembered, the Declaration of Independence and the Virginia Statute for Religious Freedom.

When it was completed, many thought the Jefferson Memorial was not the equal of the powerful Lincoln Memorial. However, it has aged gracefully in its serene setting, framed by curving groves of trees, including hundreds of cherries, and has earned its own admirers. It is a prime spot to see the cherry blossoms in bloom in spring, doubly beautiful reflected in the waters of the Tidal Basin.

Vietnam Veterans Memorial

The newest memorial on the Mall, dedicated on November 11, 1982, is not for one man but for many – the men and women of the armed forces of the United States who served in the Vietnam War. The names of the 58,156 who gave their lives and of those who remain missing are inscribed in the order they were taken from us.

The difficult requirements for the design specified

Above: *the Jefferson Memorial. The sculpture is by Rudolph Evans and the building by John Russell Pope. The walls of the Memorial bear excerpts from the Declaration of Independence and the Virginia Statute for Religious Freedom, both written by Jefferson.*

Tidal Basin water laps beside the Jefferson Memorial. The lake was dredged and land reclaimed prior to construction.

The Jefferson Memorial flanked by mature trees in high summer – the landscaping here was done by Frederick Law Olmstead, Jr. The Tidal Basin is ringed by cherry trees whose blossom complements the marble of the memorial in spring.

that the memorial must be reflective and contemplative in character, that it must harmonize with its surroundings, that it must contain the names of all who died or are listed as missing, and that it should make no overt political statement about the war. Among a flood of entries Maya Ying Lin, a twenty-one-year-old undergraduate architecture student at Yale, came up with a winning plan.

Set in a quiet, protected place that is a small park within a park, the low black granite walls are in a V, the ends pointing to the Washington and Lincoln

Memorials. The walls are 246.75 feet in length. The shiny polished surface reflects the surrounding trees, lawns, and monuments – and the people searching through the names.

The long rows of names reveal the war as a series of individual human sacrifices and ensure each name a special place in America's history. A diamond symbol shows that death is confirmed; a cross denotes those who were missing or prisoners at the end of the war. If any of the latter should return alive, a circle will be inscribed around the cross as a symbol of life.

Above: *winter rain emphasizes the poignancy of the Vietnam Memorial, a black granite wall which lies near the Lincoln Memorial on the Mall.*

Right: *a single red rose left by a mourner marks a portion of the Vietnam Veterans Memorial, inscribed with the names of the 58,000 Americans killed in the Vietnam War.*

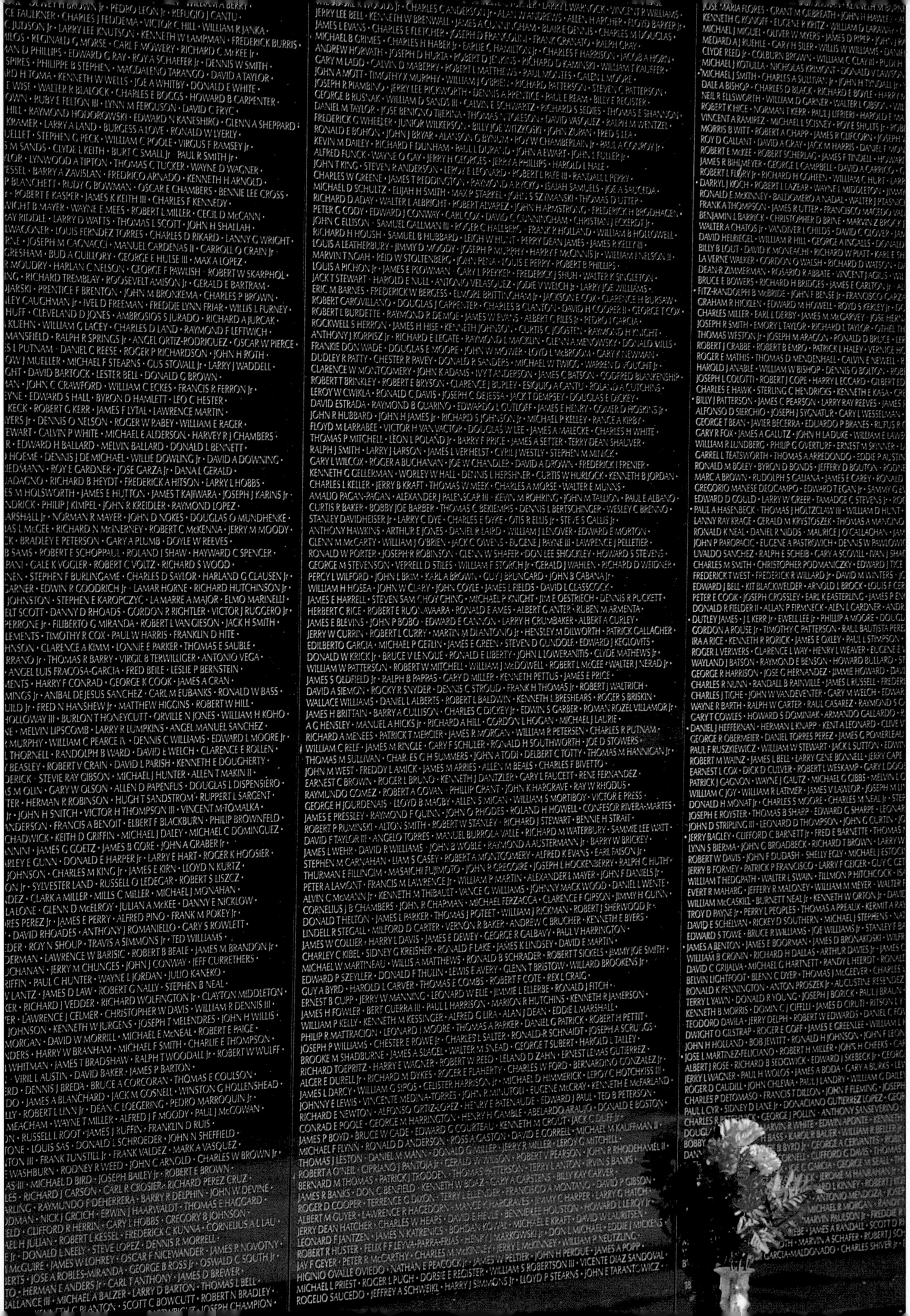

Left column

CE FAULKNER • CHARLES J FEDDEMA • PEDRO LEON Jr • REFUGIO J CANTU
CE JUDSON Jr • LARRY LEE KNUTSON • VICTOR C HILL • WILLIAM R JANKA
MILOS • REGINALD G MORSE • CARL F MOWERY • RICHARD C McKEE Jr
SPIRES • PHILIPPE B STEPHEN • MAGDALENO TARANGO • DENNIS W SMITH
RD H TOMA • KENNETH W WELLS • JOE A WHITBY • DAVID A TAYLOR
E WISE • WALTER R BLALOCK • CHARLES E BOGGS • HOWARD B CARPENTER
OWN • RUBY E FELTON III • LYNN M FERGUSON • DAVID C FRYC
HILL • RAYMOND HODOROWSKI • EDWARD N KANESHIRO • GLENN A SHEPPARD
KRAMER • LARRY A LAND • BURGESS A LOVE • RONALD W LYERLY
S M SANDS • CLYDE L KEITH • BURT C SMALL Jr • PAUL R SMITH Jr
YLOR • LYNWOOD A TIPTON • THOMAS C TUCKER • WAYNE D WAGNER
ESSEL • BARRY A ZAVISLAN • FREDRICO ARNADO • KENNETH H ARNOLD
P BLANCHETT • RUDY G BOWMAN • OSCAR E CHAMBERS • BENNIE LEE CROSS
ROBERT E KASPER • JAMES K KEITH III • CHARLES F KENNEDY
WICHT B MAYER • WAYNE E MEES • ROBERT L MILLER • CECIL D McCANN
RAY RIDDLE • LARRY D WATTS • THOMAS L SCOTT • JOHN H SHALLAH
LWAGONER • LOUIS FERNDEZ TORRES • CHARLES D RIKARD • LANNY G WRIGHT
RNE • JOSEPH M CAGNACCI • MANUEL CARDENAS Jr • CARROLL O CRAIN Jr
GRESHAM • BUD A GUILLORY • GEORGE E HULSE III • MAX A LOPEZ
MOUDRY • HARLAN C NELSON • GEORGE P PAWLISH • ROBERT W SKARPHOL
ING • RICHARD TREMBLAY • ROOSEVELT AMISON • GERALD E BARTRAM
DJARSKI • PRENTICE F BRENTON • JOHN M BRONKEMA • CHARLES F BROWN
LEY CAUGHMAN Jr • IVEL D FREEMAN • FREDDIE LYNN FRIAR • WILLIS L FURNEY
HUFF • CLEVELAND D JONES • AMBROSIOS S JURADO • RICHARD A JURCAK
KUEHN • WILLIAM G LACEY • CHARLES D LAND • RAYMOND F LEFTWICH
MANSFIELD • RALPH B SPRINGS Jr • ANGEL ORTIZ-RODRIGUEZ • OSCAR W PIERCE
S L PUTNAM • DANIEL C REESE • ROGER P RICHARDSON • JOHN H ROTH
OW J MUELLER • MICHAEL F STEARNS • GUS STOVALL Jr • LARRY J WADDELL
GHT • DAVID BARTOCK • LESTER BELL • DONALD G BROWN
MAN • JOHN C CRAWFORD • WILLIAM C ECKES • FRANCIS R FERRON Jr
EYNE • EDWARD S HALL • BYRON D HAMLETT • LEO K CHESTER
KECK • ROBERT E KERR • JAMES E LYTAL • LAWRENCE MARTIN
YERS Jr • DENNIS O NELSON • ROGER W RABEY • WILLIAM E RAGER
EWART • CALVIN P WHITE • MICHAEL E ALDERSON • HARVEY R J CHAMBERS
R • EDWARD H BALLARD • MELVIN BALLARD • DONALD L BENNETT
D HOEME • DENNIS J DE MICHAEL • WILLIE DOWLING Jr • DAVID A DOWNING
RIEDMANN • ROY E GARDNER • JOSE GARZA Jr • DANA L GERALD
UADAGNO • RICHARD B HEYDT • FREDERICK A HITSON • LARRY L HOBBS
ES M HOLSWORTH • JAMES E HUTTON • JAMES T KAJIWARA • JOSEPH J KARINS Jr
NDRICK • PHILIP J KIMPEL • JOHN R KREIDLER • RAYMOND LOPEZ
ARSHALL Jr • NORMAN R MAYER • JOHN D NOKES • DOUGLAS O MUNDHENKE
LAS L McGEE • RICHARD N McINERNEY • ROBERT C McKENNA • JERRY M MOODY
CK • BRADLEY E PETERSON • GARY A PLUMB • DOYLE W REEVES
B SAMS • ROBERT E SCHOPPAUL • ROLAND J SHAW • HAYWARD C SPENCER
PANI • GALE K VOGLER • ROBERT C VOLTZ • RICHARD S WOOD
NEN • STEPHEN P BURLINGAME • CHARLES A SAYLOR • HARLAND G CLAUSEN Jr
GARNER • EDWIN R GOODRICH Jr • LAMAR HORNE • RICHARD HUTCHINSON Jr
JOHNSTON • STEPHEN E KAROPCZYC • LA MARRE A MAJOR • ELMO MARINELLI
ELT SCOTT • DANNY D RHOADS • GORDON R RIGHTLER • VICTOR J RUGGERO Jr
PERRONE Jr • FILIBERTO G MIRANDA • ROBERT L VAN GIESON • JACK H SMITH
LEMENTS • TIMOTHY R COX • WILLY W HARRIS • FRANKLIN D HITE
HNSON • CLARENCE A KIMM • LONNIE E PARKER • THOMAS E SAUBLE
RRANO Jr • THOMAS R BARRY • VIRGIL B TERWILLIGER • ANTONIO VEGA
ANGEL LUIS FRAGOSA-GARCIA • FRED BEILE • LESLIE P BERNSTEIN
MENTS • HARRY F CONRAD • GEORGE K COOK • JAMES A CRAN
MINGS Jr • ANIBAL DE JESUS SANCHEZ • CARL M EUBANKS • RONALD W BASS
UILD Jr • FRED N HANSHEW Jr • MATTHEW HIGGINS • ROBERT W HILL
HOLLOWAY III • BURLON T HONEYCUTT • ORVILLE N JONES • WILLIAM H KOHO
NE • MELVIN LIPSCOMB • LARRY R LUMPKINS • ANGEL MANUEL SANCHEZ
MURPHY • WILLIAM C PEARCE IV • DENNIS C WILLIAMS • EDWARD L MOORE Jr
L THORNELL • RANDOLPH B WARD • DAVID E WELCH • CLARENCE E ROLLEN
Y BEASLEY • ROBERT V CRAIN • DAVID L PARISH • KENNETH E DOUGHERTY
DERICK • STEVIE RAY GIBSON • MICHAEL J HUNTER • ALLEN T MAKIN II
AS M OLIN • GARY W OLSON • ALLEN D PAPENFUS • DOUGLAS L DISPENSIERO
TER • HERMAN R ROBINSON • HUGH T SANDSTROM • RUPPERT L SARGENT
Jr • JOHN R SNITCH • VICTOR H THOMPSON III • VINCENT M TOMALKA
ANDERSON • FRANCIS A BENOIT • ELBERT F BLACKBURN • PHILIP BROWNFELD
CHADWICK • KEITH D GRIFFIN • MICHAEL J DALEY • MICHAEL C DOMINGUEZ
NINI • JAMES G GOETZ • JAMES B GORE • JOHN A GRABER Jr
ARLEY E GUNN • DONALD E HARPER Jr • LARRY E HART • ROGER K HOOSIER
JOHNSON • CHARLES M KING Jr • JAMES E KIRN • LLOYD N KURTZ
ON Jr • SYLVESTER LAND • RUSSELL O LEDEGAR • ROBERT S LISZCZ
NDEZ • CLARK A MILLER • MILLS C MILLER • MICHAEL J MONAHAN
LALONE • GLENN D McELROY • JULIAN A McKEE • DANNY E NICKLOW
RES PEREZ Jr • JAMES E PERRY • ALFRED PINO • FRANK M POKEY Jr
DAVID RHOADES • ANTHONY J ROMANIELLO • GARY S ROWLETT
DER • ROY N SHOUP • TRAVIS A SIMMONS Jr • TED WILLIAMS
ERMAN • LAWRENCE W BARISIC • ROBERT B BEALE • JAMES M BRANDON Jr
UCHANAN • JERRY M CHUNGES • JOHN J CONWAY • JEFF CURRETHERS
RIFFIN • PAUL C HUNTER • WAYNE L JORDAN • JULIO KANEKO
V LANTZ • JAMES D LAW • ROBERT G NALLY • STEPHEN B NEAL
KER • RICHARD J VEDDER • RICHARD WOLFINGTON Jr • CLAYTON MIDDLETON
ER • LAWRENCE J CELMER • CHRISTOPHER W DAVIS • WILLIAM R DENNIS III
JOHNSON • KENNETH W JURGENS • JOSEPH T MELENDRES • JOHN H WILLIS
MORGAN • DAVID W MORRILL • MICHAEL E McNEAL • ROBERT E PAIGE
NDERS • HARRY W BRANHAM • WILLIAM F SMITH • CHARLIE E THOMPSON
WHITMAN • JAMES T BRADSHAW • RALPH T WOODALL Jr • ROBERT W WULFF
VIRIL L AUSTIN • DAVID BAKER • JAMES P BARTON
RD • DENNIS J BREDA • BRUCE A CORCORAN • THOMAS E COULSON
DO • JAMES A BLANCHARD • JACK M GOSNELL • WINSTON D HOLLENSHEAD
LLY • ROBERT L LINN Jr • DEAN C LOEGERING • PEDRO MARROQUIN Jr
MEACHAM • WAYNE T MILLER • ALFRED J F MOODY • PAUL J McGOWAN
N • RUSSELL L ROOT • JAMES J RUFFIN • FRANKLIN D RUIS
TONE • LOUIS SAS • DONALD L SCHROEDER • JOHN N SHEFFIELD
LTON III • FRANK TUNSTILL Jr • FRANK VALDEZ • MARK A VASQUEZ
WASHBURN • RODNEY R WEED • JOHN C ARNOLD • ROBERT E BROWN
AS III • MICHAEL D BIRD • JOSEPH BAILEY Jr
LEE • RICHARD J CARSON • CARL R CROSIER • RICHARD PEREZ CRUZ
ARLING • RAYMUNDO F DEHERRERA • BARRY R DELPHIN • JOHN W DEVINE
ODMAN • NICK J GRCICH • ERWIN J HAARVALDT • THOMAS E HAGGARD
ELD • CLIFFORD R HERRIN • GARY L HOBBS • GREGORY B JOHNSON
AEL H JULIAN • ROBERT E KESSEL • FREDERICK C KUNNA • CORNELIUS A LAU
Jr • DONALD J NEELY • STEVE LOPEZ • DENNIS R MORRELL
McGUIRE • JAMES W LOHREY • OSCAR E NICEWANDER • JAMES J NOVOTNY
BERTS • JOSE A ROBLES-MIRANDA • GEORGE B ROSS Jr • OSWALD C SOUTH II
TO • HERMAN E ANDERS Jr • CARL ANTHONY • JAMES D BREWER
BALLANCE III • MICHAEL A BALZER • LARRY D BARTON • ROBERT N BRADLEY
TH C BLANTON • SCOTT C BOWCUTT • JOSEPH CHAMPION

Center column

ER IN WOOD Jr • JAMES C ANDERSON Jr • ALAN W ANDREWS • LARRY L WARNOCK • VINCENT R WILLIAMS
JERRY LEE BELL • KENNETH W BRENWALL • JAMES A CUNNINGHAM • ALLEN H ARCHER • FLOYD BARKER Jr
JAMES J EVANS • CHARLES E FLETCHER • JOSEPH D FRANCOLINI • FRANK GRANATO • CHARLES M DOUGLAS Jr
MICHAEL B GRIMES • CHARLES H HABER Jr • EARLIE C HAMILTON Jr • CHARLES F HARRISON • RALPH GRAY
ANDREW HORVATH • JOSEPH D HURTA • RICHARD D JENKINS • RICHARD D KAMINSKI • JACOB A HORN
GARY M LADD • CALVIN D MABERRY • ROBERT D MATTHEWS • RICHARD D KAMINSKI • WILLIAM T KAUFFER
JOHN A MOTT • TIMOTHY X MURPHY • WILLIAM J O'BRIEN • RAUL MONTES • CALVIN MOORE
JOSEPH P PIAMBINO • JERRY LEE PICKWORTH • WILLIAM J O'BRIEN • RICHARD PATTERSON • STEVEN C PATTERSON
GEORGE B RUSNAK • WILLIAM D SANDS III • CALVIN E SCHWARTZ • DENNIS A PRENTICE • PAUL E REAM • BILLY E REGISTER
DANIEL M TAYLOR • JOSE BENIGNO TIJERINA • THOMAS L TOLESON • DAVID VASQUEZ • RALPH M WENTZEL
FREDERICK G WHEELER • JUNIOR WILKERSON • BILLY JOE WITZKOSKI • JOHN ZUPAN • FRED S LEA
RONALD E BOHON • JOHN J BRYAR • ALANSON G BYNUM • ROY W CHAMBERLAIN Jr • PAUL A CONROY Jr
KEVIN M DAILEY • RICHARD F DUNHAM • PAUL L DURAN • JOHN A EWART • JOHN L FULLER Jr
ALFRED FUNCK • WAYNE O GAY • JERRY H GEORGES • JERRY A PHILLIPS • HAROLD L HALE
JOHN T KING • STEVEN R ANDERSON • LEROY E LEONARD • ROBERT L PATE III • RANDALL L PERRY
CHARLES W GREENE • JAMES T REDDINGTON • RAYMOND A RYCKO • ISAIAH SAMUELS • JOE A SAUCEDA
MICHAEL D SCHULTZ • ELIJAH H SMITH • MAX P STARPEL • JOHN S SZYMANSKI • THOMAS D UTTER
RICHARD D ADAY • WALTER L ALBRIGHT • MARGARET J • JOHN H ARMSTRONG • FREDERICK H BRODHAGEN
PETER G CODY • EDWARD J CONWAY • CARL COX • DAVID C CUNNINGHAM • CHRISTIAN J ECKERDT Jr
JOHN C ELLISON • SAMUEL GALLMAN III • ROGER C HALLBERG • FRANK P HOLLAND • WILLIAM A HOLLOWELL
RICHARD H HOUSH • SAMUEL B HUBBARD • LEIGH W HUNT • PERRY DEAN JAMES • JAMES R KELLY III
LOUIS A LEATHERBURY • JIMMY D MOODY • JOSEPH P MURPHY • HARVEY F McGINNIS Jr • WILLIAM I NELSON II
MARVIN T NOAH • REID W STOLTENBERG • JOHN PENA • LOUIS E PERRY • ROBERT B PHILLIPS
LOUIS A PICHON Jr • JAMES E PLOWMAN • GARY L PREKKER • FREDERICK J SHUH • WALTER K SINGLETON
JACK T STEWART • HAROLD E NULL • ANTONIO VELASQUEZ • JODIE V WELCH Jr • LARRY LEE WILLIAMS
ERIC M BARNES • FREDERICK W BERGESS • ELMORE BRITTINGHAM Jr • JACKSON E COX • CLARENCE H BURSAW
ROBERT CAROVILLANO • DOUGLAS J CARPENTER • CHARLES B CLANTON • DAVID H COOPER II • GEORGE T COX
ROBERT L BURDETTE • RAYMOND R DEMOE • JAMES W EVANS • ALBERT C FILES Jr • PEDRO J GARCIA
ROCKWELL S HERRON • JAMES H HISE • KENNETH JOHNSON • CURTIS C JOOSTEN • RAYMOND H KNIGHT
ANTHONY J KORPISZ Jr • RICHARD E LEGATE • RAYMOND C MACKLIN • GLENN A MENOWSKY • DONALD MILLS
FRANKIE DON WADE • DOUGLAS E MOORE • JOHN W MOWER • LOYD L McBROOM • GARY K NEWMAN
DUDLEY PATTY • CHESTER R PAVEY • DONALD R SANDERS • MICHAEL W TWIGG • WARREN D VOUGHT Jr
CLARENCE W MONTGOMERY • JOHN K ADAMS • IVY A DEPSON • JAMES C BATSON • GEORGE BLANKENSHIP
ROBERT T BRINKLEY • ROBERT E BRYSON • CLARENCE J BUPLEY • ESIQUIO A CANTU • ROLAND A CUTCHINS
LEROY W CWIKLA • RONALD C DAVIS • JOSEPH C DE JESSA • JACK T DEMPSEY • DOUGLAS E DICKEY
DAVID ESTRADA • RAYMOND B GUARINO • EDWARDO L GUTLOFF • JAMES E HENRY • GOMER D HOSKINS Jr
JOHN R HUBBARD • JOHN H JAMES Jr • RICHARD S JOHNSON Jr • MICHAEL P KELLEY • RANCE A KIRBY
FLOYD M LARRABEE • VICTOR H VAN VACTOR • DOUGLAS W LEE • JAMES A MALECKE • CHARLES H WHITE
THOMAS P MITCHELL • LEON L POLAND Jr • BARRY F PRICE • JAMES A SETTER • TERRY DEAN SHALVER
RALPH J SMITH • LARRY J LARSON • JAMES L VER HELST • CYRIL J WESTLY • STEPHEN M MINICK
GARY L WILCOX • ROGER A BUCHANAN • JOE W CHANDLER • DAVID A DROWN • FREDERICK I FRENIER
KENNETH G GELLERMAN • WORLEY W HALL • DENNIS L HEPSHINGER • CLYDE W HURLOCK • KENNETH B JORDAN
CHARLES L KELLER • JERRY B KRAFT • THOMAS W MEEK • CHARLES A MORSE • WALTER E MUNNS
AMALIO PAGAN-PAGAN • ALEXANDER J PALENSCAR III • KEVIN M ROHRING • JOHN M TALLON • PAULE ALBANO
CURTIS R BAKER • BOBBY JOE BARBER • THOMAS C BERKEMPIS • JAMES E BERTSCHINGER • WESLEY C BRENNO
STANLEY DAVIDHEISER Jr • LARRY C DYE • CHARLES E DYKE • OTIS R ELLIS Jr • STEVE S GALLIS Jr
ANTHONY HAWKINS • ARTHUR E JONES • DANIEL R LAIRD • WILLIAM J LENOVER • EDWARD E MORTON
GLENN M McCARTY • WILLIAM J O'BRIEN • JACK C OWENS • GLENN E PAYNE III • LAWRENCE J PELLETIER
RONALD W PORTER • JOSEPH R ROBINSON • GLENN W SHAFER • DON LEE SHOCKLEY • HOWARD S STEVENS
GEORGE M STEVENSON • VEPRELL D STILES • WILLIAM F STORCH Jr • GERALD J WAHLEN • RICHARD D WEIDNER
PERCY L WILFORD • JOHN L BRIM • KARL A BROWN • GUY J BRUNGARD • JOHN B CABANA Jr
WILLIAM H HOSEA • JOHN W CLARY • JOHN COYLE • JAMES L FIELDS • DAVID L CLASSCOCK
JAMES H HARRELL • STEVEN SAM CHOY CHING • MICHAEL P KNIGHT • JIM E OESTREICH • DENNIS R PUCKETT
HERBERT C RICE • ROBERT E RUONAVAARA • RONALD E AMES • ALBERT G ANTER • RUBEN M ARMENTA
JAMES E BLEVINS • JOHN P BOBO • EDWARD E CANNON • LARRY H CRUMBAKER • ALBERT A CURLEY
JERRY W CURRIN • ROBERT L CURRY • MARTIN M DIANTONIO Jr • HENSLEY M DILLWORTH • PATRICK GALLAGHER
EDILBERTO GARCIA • MICHAEL P GETLIN • JAMES E GREEN • STEVEN D GUNDOLE • EDWARD J KEGLOVITS
DONALD W KRICK Jr • BRUCE V LE NOUE • RONALD E LIBERTY • JOHN L LOWERANITIS • CLYDE MATHEWS Jr
WILLIAM W PATTERSON • ROBERT W MITCHELL • WILLIAM J McDOWELL • ROBERT M McGEE • WALTER J NERAD Jr
JAMES S OLDFIELD Jr • RALPH B PAPPAS • GARY D MILLER • KENNETH PETTUS • JAMES E PRICE
DAVID A SIEMON • ROCKY R SNYDER • DENNIS C STROUD • FRANK H THOMAS Jr • ROBERT J WALTRICH
WALLACE WILLIAMS • DANIEL L ALBERTS • ROBERT L BALDWIN • KENNETH L BRESHEARS • ROGER S BRISKIN
JAMES H BRITTAIN • BARRY A CULLISON • CHARLES C DICKEY Jr • EDWIN S GARBER • ROMAN ROZEL VILLAMOR Jr
A G HENSLEY • MANUEL A HICKS Jr • RICHARD A HILL • GORDON L HOGAN • MICHAEL J LAURIE
RICHARD A MENEES • PATRICK T MERCIER • JAMES R MORGAN • WILLIAM R PETERSEN • CHARLES R PUTNAM
WILLIAM C RELF • JAMES M RINGLE • GARY F SCHULER • RONALD H SOUTHWORTH • JOE D STOWERS
THOMAS M SULLIVAN • CHAR-LES G H SUMMERS • JOHN A TODI • DELBERT C TOTTY • THOMAS M HANNIGAN Jr
JOHN M WEST • FREDDY L AMICK • JAMES M ARRIES • ALLEN M BEALS • CHARLES F BIVETTO
EARNEST C BROWN • ROGER E BRUNO • KENNETH J DANTZLER • GARY L FAUCETT • RENE FERNANDEZ
RAYMUNDO GOMEZ • ROBERT A COVAN • PHILLIP GRANT • JOHN K HARGRAVE • RAY W RHODUS
GEORGE H JOURDENAIS • LLOYD B MAGBY • ALLEN S MICAN • JAMES S MORTIBOY • VICTOR E PRESS
JAMES E PRESSLEY • RAYMOND F QUINN • JOHN O RHODES • ROLAND H HOWELL • CONFESOR RIVERA-MARTES
ROBERT P RUMINSKI • ALTON SMITH • ROBERT W STANLEY • RICHARD J STEWART • BENNIE H STRAIT
DAVID F TAYLOR III • ANGELO TORRES • MANUEL BURROLA VALLE • RICHARD M WATERBURY • SAMMIE LEE WATT
JAMES L WEHR • DAVID R WILLIAMS • JOHN B WOBLE • RAYMOND A AUSTERMANN Jr • BARRY W BRICKEY
STEPHEN M CARNAHAN • LIAM S CASEY • ROBERT A MONTGOMERY • ALFRED K EVANS • EARL FAISON Jr
THURMAN E FILLINGIM • MASAICHI FUJIMOTO • JOHN P GREGOIRE • JOSEPH E HOCKENBERRY • RALPH C HUTH Jr
PETER A LAMONT • FRANCIS M LAWRENCE Jr • WILLIAM P MARTIN • ALEXANDER L MAYER • JOHN F DANIELS Jr
ALVIN C McMANN Jr • KENNETH M THIBAULT • VANCE G WILLIAMS • JIMMY MACKWOOD • DANIEL L WENTE
CORNELIUS J B CHAMBERS • JOHN R CHAPMAN • MICHAEL FERZACCA • CLARENCE F GIPSON • JIMMY H GUNN
DONALD T HELTON • JAMES L PARKER • THOMAS J POTEET • WILLIAM J RICKMAN • ROBERT J SHERWOOD Jr
LINDELL R STEGALL • MILFORD D CARTER • VERNON R BAKER • ANDREW C BRUCHER • KENNETH E BYERS
JAMES W COLLIER • HARRY L DAVIS • JAMES E DEWEY • GEORGE R GALBAVY • PAUL V HARRINGTON
CHARLEY C KIBEL • SIDNEY G KREISHER • RONALD F LAKE • JAMES K LINDSEY • DAVID E MARTIN
MICHAEL W MARTINEAU • WILLIS A MATTHEWS • RONALD B SCHRADER • ROBERT SICKELS • JIMMY JOE SMITH
EDWARD P SZEYLLER • JAMES D THULIN • LEWIS E AVERY • GLENN W BRISTOW • WILLARD BROOKENS Jr
GUY A BYRD • HAROLD L CARVER • THOMAS E COMBS • ROBERT F COTE • REX L CRAIG
ERNEST B CUPP • JERRY W MANNING • LEONARD W ELIE • JIMMIE L ELLERBE • RONALD J FITCH
JAMES H FOWLER • BERT GUERRA III • PAUL L HARRISON • MARION R HUTCHINS • KENNETH R JAMERSON
WILLIAM P KELLY • KENNETH M KESSINGER • ALFRED G LIRA • ALAN J DEAN • ESTEB L MARSHALL
PHILIP R MATTRACION • LEONARD I MOORE • THOMAS A PARKER • DANIEL G PATRICK • ROBERT H PETTIT
JOSEPH P WILLIAMS • CHESTER E ROWE Jr • CHARLES L SALTER • RONALD R SCHNAIDT • JOSEPH A SCRUGGS
BROOKE M SHADBURNE • JAMES A SLAGEL • ROBERT W REED • LELAND D ZAHN • ERNEST LEMAS GUTIERREZ
RICHARD TOEPRITZ • HARRY E WAGNER • CHARLES W FORD • BERNARDINO GONZALEZ Jr
ALGER E DURELL Jr • RAYMOND M DYKES • ROGER E FLAHERTY • JOHN J HIMMERICK • GEORGE P HOTCHKISS III
JAMES L DARCY • WILLIAM G SIPOS • CELISTER HARRISON Jr • EUGENE McCRAY • KENNETH E McFARLAND
JOHNNY E LEWIS • VINCENTE MEDINA-TORRES • JOHN P MINUTOLI • EUGENE McCRAY • EDWARD J PAUL • TED B PETERSON
RICHARD E NEWTON • ALFONSO ORTIZ-LOPEZ • HENRY H GAMBLE • ABELARDO ARAUJO • DONALD E BOSTON Jr
CONRAD E POOLE • GEORGE M HARRINGTON • KENNETH M CROUT • DAVID E CORRELL • MICHAEL M KAUFFMAN II
JAMES P BOYD • BRUCE W CADE • EDWARD G COURTEAU • KENNETH M CROUT • JACK C DUFFE Jr
MICHAEL P FLYNN • RONALD D ANDERSON • ROSS A GASTON • JERRY R MILLER • LEROY G MITCHELL
THOMAS J LESTON • DANIEL M MANN • DONALD G MILLER • ROBERT PEARSON • JOHN C RHODEHAMEL II
ROBERTA O'NEIL • CIPRIANO J PANTOJA Jr • GERALD W WILSON • TERRY L ANTON • IRVIN S BANKS
BERNARD M THOMAS • PATRICK J TRODDEN • THOMAS W STERNS • BILLY KAY CARTER
JAMES R BANKS • DON G BENFIELD • KENNETH W BOAZ • FRANCISCO A MONTANO • DAVID P GIBSON
ROGER D COOPER • TERRENCE G DIXON • TERRY L BELCHER • JAMES V HARPER • LARRY D HATCH
ALBERT M GUYER • LAWRENCE R HAGEDORN • DAVID H HARGRAVES • BENNIE LEE HOUSTON • RONALD L LEROY Jr
JERRY DEAN HATCHER • CHARLES W HEAPS • DAVID H HARGRAVES • MICHAEL E KRAFT • DAVID W LAURITSEN
LEONARD R JANTZEN • JAMES X KATRENICS • RONALD RAY MARTZ • HENRY J MARKOWSKI Jr • WILLIAM P NEUTZLING
ROBERT R HUSTER • FELIX F F LEYVA-PARRARTAS • JAMES W PELTIER • JOHN H PERDUE • JAMES A PROPP
JAY F GEYER • PETER R McCARTHY • CHARLES • JAMES W PELTIER • JOHN H PERDUE • VICENTE DIAZ SANDOVAL
HIGINO OVALLE OVIEDO • NATHAN E PEACOCK • GEORGE E REGISTER • WILLIAM S ROBERTSON III • JOHN E TARANTOWICZ
MICHAEL L PRIEST • ROGER L PUGH • DORSIE E REGISTER • LLOYD P STEARNS • JOHN E TARANTOWICZ
ROGELIO SAUCEDO • JEFFREY A SCHWEIKL • HARRY J SIMMONS Jr

Right column

JOSE MARIA FLORES • GRANT M GILBREATH • JOHN H HAWLE...
KENNETH G RONGFF • EUGENE H KURTZ • WILLIAM D LARAWA...
MICHAEL J MIGUEL • OLIVER W MYERS • JAMES D PIPER • JOH...
MEDARD A J RUEHLE • GARY M SILER • WILLIS W OBANDON...
CLYDE REED Jr • COLBURN BROWN • WILLIAM C CLAY II • PUE...
MICHAEL J KOTULLA • NICHOLAS KRIMONT • DANIEL V LEWI...
MICHAEL J SMITH • CHARLES A SULLIVAN • JOHN H TYNDALL...
DALE A BISHOP • CHARLES D BLACK • FRANCIS E BOYLE • HARRY...
NEIL R ELLSWORTH • WILLIAM D GARVER • WALTER L GIBSO...
ROBERT B HICE • NORMAN T KERR • PAUL J LIFRIERI • HAROLD...
VINCENT A RAMIREZ • MICHAEL J SCISNEY • FOYE SHULTS Jr...
MORRIS B WITT • JAMES R CLIFCORN • JOSEPH...
ROY D GALLANT • DAVID A GRAY • JACK M HARRIS • DANIEL F...
ROBERT E McKEE • ROBERT SCHERLAG • JAMES F TINDELL • H...
JAMES R BIHLMEYER • GEORGE L CAMPBELL • DAVID A CARRICO...
ROBERT E FLURY Jr • RICHARD H GOHEEN • WILLIAM C HURT...
DARRYL J KOCH • ROBERT E LAZEAR • WAYNE L MIDDLETON...
RONALD E McKINNEY • BALDOMERO A NADAL • WESLEY J PTASNIK...
FRANK A THOMPSON • JAMES R UTTER • FRANCISCO MACEDO VA...
BENJAMIN L BARRICK • CHRISTOPHER D BRINE • MARVIN Z BROCK...
WALTER A CHATOS Jr • VANDIVER L CHILDS • DAVID C GLOVER...
DAVID HELRIEGEL • WILLIAM R HILL • GEORGE A INGALLS • DONAL...
BILLY B LOUT • DAVID K MONEACHI • RICHARD W PLATT • KARL E...
LA VERNE WALKER • GORDON O WALSH • RICHARD D WATSON Jr...
DEAN-R ZIMMERMAN • ROSARIO R ABBATE • VINCENT J AGUL...
BRUCE A BOWERS • RICHARD H BRIDGES • JAMES E CARLTON Jr...
FITZ-RANDOLPH B McBRIDE • JOHN F BENSE Jr • FRANCISCO G PAZ...
GRAHAM B HICKLEN • EDWARD H HOWELL • FLOYD S KERLEY Jr...
CHARLES MILLER • EARL L DERBY • JAMES M McGARVEY • JOSE HERN...
JOSEPH R SMITH • EMORY L TAYLOR • RICHARD L TAYLOR • OTHEL TH...
THOMAS WESTON Jr • JOSEPH M ARAGON • RONALD D BRUCE • LEO...
ROBERT J CRABBE • ROBERT B EMRO • PATRICK L HALEY • VERNICE HO...
ROGER E MATHIS • THOMAS D MENDENHALL • CALVIN E NEWELL...
HAROLD J ANABLE • WILLIAM W BISHOP • DENNIS O BOLTON • ROBI...
JOSEPH L COLOTTI • ROBERT J COPE • HARRY L LECCARD • GILBERT ED...
CHARLES E HAWK • STERLING C HENDRICKS • KENNETH E KASA-ZER...
BILLY J PATTERSON • JAMES C PEARSON • LARRY RAY REEVES • JAMES...
ALFONSO D SIERCHIO • JOSEPH J SYGNATUR • GARY L WESSELMAN...
GEORGE T BEAN • JAVIER BECERRA • EDUARDO P BRANES • RUFUS R O...
GARY R FOX • JAMES A GALUTZ • JOHN H LADUKE • WILLIAM E LAWSO...
WILLIAM R LUNDBERG • PHILIP G OVERTURF • ERNEST M SKINNER Jr...
CARRELL L TEATSWORTH • THOMAS A ARREDONDO • EDDIE P AUSTIN...
RONALD M BOLEY • BYRON D BONDS • DILFORD J BOUTON • ROBER...
MARC A BROWN • RUDOLPH S GALIANA • JAMES E CAREY • RONALD...
GREGORIO MANESE DEOCAMPO • EDMOND E TEGAN Jr • SAMMY G AN...
EDWARD D GOULD • LARRY W GREER • TAMADGE C STEVENS Jr • RON...
PAUL A MANGES • THOMAS J HOLTZCLAW III • WILLIAM D HUNT...
LANNY RAY KRAGE • GERALD M KRYSTOSZEK • THOMAS A MANGINO...
RONALD K NEAL • DANIEL P NIDDS • MAURICE J O'CALLAGHAN • JAM...
JOHN P PAROBECIC • EUGENE A PASTROVICH • DENNIS W PAWLOWSKI...
UVALDO SANCHEZ • RALPH E SCHEIB • GARY A SCOVILL • IVAN J SHAO...
CHARLES M SMITH • CHRISTOPHER PODMANICZKY • EDWARD J TICE...
FREDERICK TWEST • FREDERICK R WILLARD Jr • DAVID M WINTERS...
EDWARD J BELL • KIT BLACKWELDER • ARNOLD L BROCK • LOUIS F CER...
PETER E COOK • JOSEPH CROSSLEY • EARL K EASTERLING • JAMES P EV...
DONALD R FIELDER II • ALLAN P FIRMENICK • ALEN L CARDNER • ANDR...
DUTLEY JAMES • J L KERR Jr • EWELL LEE Jr • PHILLIP A MOORE • DOL GL...
GORDON A ROUSE Jr • TIMOTHY C PATTERSON • RAUL BAUTISTA PERE...
IRA A RICE • KENNETH R RORICK • JAMES E OXLEY • PAUL L STIMPSON...
ROGER CLARENCE L WAY • HENRY L WEAVER • EUGENE E...
WAYLAND J BATSON • RAYMOND E BENSON • HOWARD BULLARD • ST...
GEORGE R HARRISON • JOSE G HERNANDEZ • JIMMIE HOWARD • DAV...
CHARLES R NUNN • RANDALL B RAINVILLE • JAMES L RUSSELL • FREDER...
CHARLES J TIGHE • JOHN W VANDEVENTER • GARY M WELCH • EDWAR...
WAYNE R BARTH • RALPH W CARTER • RAUL CASAREZ • RAYMOND S C...
GARY T COWLES • HOWARD S DOMINIAK • ARMANDO GALLARDO Jr...
DANIEL J HEFFERNAN • HERMAN L KNAPP • KENT A LEONARD • CLIVE W...
GEORGE OBERMEIER • DANIEL TORRES PEREZ • JAMES G POMERLEAU...
PAUL F RUSZKIEWICZ • WILLIAM W STEWART • JACK L SUTTON • D...
ROBERT M WAINZ • JAMES L BELL • LARRY GENE BOMANI • JERRY CAPE...
EARNEST L COX • DICK D CULVER • ROBERT L WESKAMP • GARY L DOO...
PATRICK J GAGNON • WAYNE J GAUTZ • MICHAEL G GIBBS • MELVIN L C...
WILLIAM C JOY • WILLIAM R LATIMER • JAMES V LAWLOR • JOSEPH H LIT...
DONALD H MONAT Jr • CHARLES S MOORE • CHARLES M NEAL Jr • STEVE...
JOSEPH E ROYSTER • THOMAS B SHARP • EDWARD G SHARPE • LEONAR...
JOHN D STRIPLING III • LEONARD D THOMPSON • JOHN G CURTIN • JO...
JERRY BAGLEY • CLIFFORD C BARNETT • FRED E BARNETTE • THOMAS...
LYNN S BIERMA • GEORGE W BROADBECK • RICHARD T BROWN • LARRY W...
ROBERT W DAVIS • JOHN F DUDASH • SHELBY EGLY • MICHAEL J ESTOCI...
JERRY B FORMEY • PATRICK P FRANCISCO • JERRY F GEICER • GUY C GET...
WILLIAM T HEDGPATH • WALTER L SWAIN • TILLMON P HITCHCOCK • IS...
EVERT R MAHARG • JEFFREY R MALONEY • WILLIAM M WEVER • WALTER P...
WILLIAM McCASKILL • BURNETT NEAL Jr • KENNETH W ORTON Jr • DAVID...
TROY D PAYNE Jr • PERRY L PEOPLES • THOMAS A PREAUX • KERMIT A RA...
DAVID E SCHELVAN • RICKEY D SOUTHERN • MICHAEL J STEPHENS • NA...
EDWARD S TOWE • BRUCE R WILLIAMS • JOE WILLIAMS Jr • STANLEY F BA...
JAMES A BENTON • JAMES E BOORMAN • JAMES D BRONARDSKI • WILFR...
WILLIAM B DIXON • RICHARD H DALLAS • ARTHUR DAWES Jr • JAMES E...
DAVID C GRIJALVA • MICHAEL G HARTNETT • RANDY L HEERDT • CHARLES...
BELVIN LIGHTFOOT • GLENN C DYER • THOMAS J McGEAVER • CHARLES...
RONALD K PENNINGTON • ANTON PROSZEK Jr • AUGUSTINE REZENDEZ...
TERRY L YAWN • DONALD R YOUNG • JOSEPH J BORICK • PAUL J BRAUN...
KENNETH B MORRIS • DOMINIC J CIFELLI • JAMES D CIRUTI • RITSON L...
TEODORO DAVILA • JERRY DELPH • ROBERT W EDWARDS • DANIEL C FOW...
DWIGHT O GILSTRAP • GEORGE E GREENLEE • JAMES E GREENLEE • WILLIAM L...
JOHN H GALLUP • BOB JEWITT • RONALD H JOHNSON • JOHN H CHEEKS III...
JOSE L MARTINEZ-FELICIANO • ROBERT H MILLER • JOHN H CHEEKS III...
ALBERT H ROSE • RICHARD B SEDGWICK • EDWARD J SKEBECK Jr • CHARLES...
JERRY L WAGNER • PAUL H WOLOS • JAMES A BODA • GARY A BURKS • LA...
ROGER D CAUDILL • JOHN CHLEWA • PAUL J LANDRY • WILLIAM A DAILE...
CHARLES P DETOMASO • FRANCIS J DILLON • JOHN F FLEMING • JOSEPH...
PAUL L CYR • SIDNEY D LANE Jr • DONACIANO GUTIERREZ LOPEZ • JE...
DOUG... • GEORGE J POLLIN • ANTHONY SANSEVERINO...
WHITE • JEROME APONTE • KENNETH...
BOBBY... • KAROLR BAUER • WINFRED A BEELER Jr...
B BASS • GEORGE A CERVANTES • THOMAS...
DAN... CLIFFORD G DAVIS • THOMAS...

Above: *a National Park Service man tends the Vietnam Veterans Memorial. Personal offerings left at the foot of the wall are put into storage.*

Facing page: *a bunch of flowers shines out beside the somber granite of the Vietnam Veterans Memorial. Somewhere, someone is remembered.*

Right: *a solitary mourner stands in the rain in front of a granite panel of the Vietnam Veterans Memorial that bears a name significant to him.*

A life-size sculpture, *The Three Servicemen*, plus an American flag flying from a sixty-foot staff were added to the memorial in 1984.

This simplest yet most moving of monuments was created as a tangible symbol of healing for the most divisive and controversial war in the nation's history.

Facing page: *the Navy and Marine Memorial on Columbia Island in the Potomac. These simple gulls are unforgettable.*

Above: *the Peace Monument on Pennsylvania Avenue, a marble memorial to sailors slain in the Civil War.*

Right: *the Peace Memorial, close to the Capitol. The figure of America is depicted weeping on the shoulder of History.*

Other Memorials

A city where old times are not forgotten, Washington has many memorials other than the major ones. It seems fitting that the official monument to Theodore Roosevelt, an outdoorsman, be located on a forested island close to the heart of the city. Near an imposing bronze figure of Roosevelt are tablets engraved with excerpts from his writings.

The Lyndon Baines Johnson Memorial, dedicated in 1974, is a rough-hewn nineteen-foot slab of Texas granite in a garden setting along the George Washington Memorial Parkway, not far from the Pentagon. Nearby is the Navy-Marine Memorial, a graceful vision of gulls in flight over crashing waves that is a riverside monument to those who died at sea during World War I.

One of the least conspicuous of the monuments is the Franklin Roosevelt Memorial, a marble block in a grassy triangle facing Pennsylvania Avenue. The president himself chose the site and the form. In 1980, Congress passed a law assigning a prominent location for a larger monument in East Potomac Park near the Jefferson Memorial. A creative design has been done, but to date no money has been appropriated. If congressional history repeats itself, the monument should be completed in about fifty years.

There is a bit of irony to the timing of two new memorials under construction – a German-American Friendship Garden, at the approach to the Washington Monument, and the United States Holocaust Memorial Museum memorializing the Nazi annihilation of six million Jews.

Washington's Squares and Statues

L'Enfant's pattern of sweeping avenues intersected with spacious squares and circles was successful in making the city a grand showcase also for statuary. Though the growth of trees has obscured the open views he intended, the overall patterns remain,

Above: *the Grant Memorial at the foot of the Capitol lawn.*

Facing page: *speckles of colored light from stained-glass windows fall on a statue of a grim Washington in Washington Cathedral.*

adorned with statues that pay tribute to a number of American heroes as well as a few foreign friends and defenders, a virtual "Who's Who" in American history.

Marquis de Lafayette, who sided with the U.S. in its war for Independence, presides over the square that was named for him, just opposite the White House. His neighbor in Lafayette Park is General Andrew Jackson, shown on horseback reviewing his troops at the battle of New Orleans.

Christopher Columbus, who discovered America, stands tall in front of Union Station poised on the bow of a ship with a winged figurehead below. Outstanding among the many statues of George Washington are two at the Washington Cathedral, one on horseback and another portraying him walking down the aisle at Christ Church. Benjamin Franklin, our first postmaster, is appropriately placed in the courtyard of the newly renovated Old Post Office Pavilion, while Daniel Webster, the nation's champion debater, is

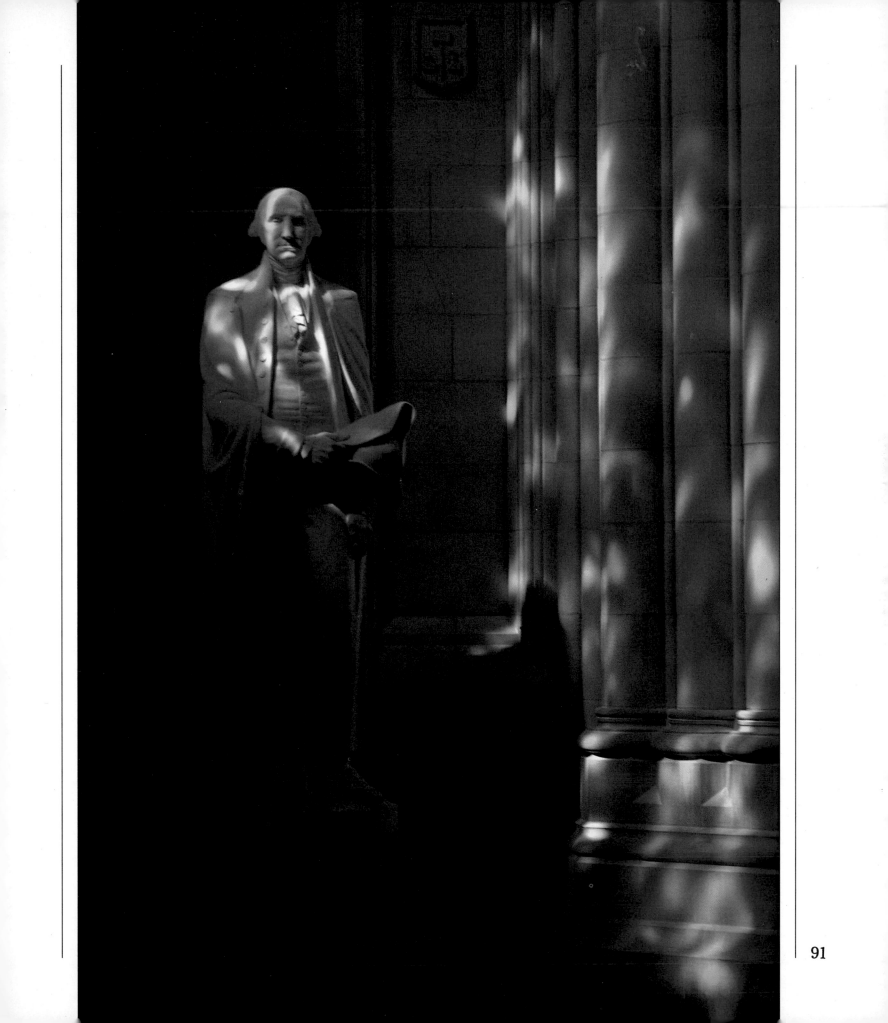

Left: *Grant Square, where the centerpiece is an imposing bronze and marble equestrian statue of Ulysses S. Grant.*

Below: *Arlington Memorial Bridge. Completed in 1932 this connects the Lincoln Memorial to Arlington National Cemetery.*

posted prominently at Massachusetts Avenue, between Sixteenth and Seventeenth Streets. Sir Winston Churchill, America's staunch British ally in World War II, also resides on Massachusetts Avenue, standing nine feet tall on the British Embassy property. One of the few outdoor life-size statues of Abraham Lincoln can be seen in Judiciary Square.

No log of statues is complete without war heroes. Brigadier General Count Casimer Pulaski, who joined the American struggle for independence, is at Pennsylvania Avenue and Thirteenth Street, while

naval hero, Commodore John Paul Jones, stands in West Potomac Park. General Philip H. Sheridan, leader of the Union Cavalry, is honored at Sheridan Circle, and General John J. Pershing, World War I General of the Armies, is portrayed in Pershing Square.

An imposing seventeen-foot bronze and marble statue of Ulysses S. Grant astride a horse can be seen at Grant Square, but an even more impressive Grant memorial is at the eastern end of the Mall, at the foot of the Capitol lawn. It shows the General presiding over a battle scene, a tableau of seven cavalrymen

charging into battle along with an artillery troop with three horses hauling cannon. The work by Henry Merwin Shrady, the largest cast sculpture in the country at the time, was begun in 1901 and took two decades to complete. The sculptor died two weeks before the dedication of his work in April 1922.

Also notable among the many sculptures in the capital are the Memorial Bridge Equestrian Statues, cast in Italy and surfaced in pure gold. They were a gift from the Italian nation to the United States in 1951.

Light from the Capitol silhouettes the Grant Memorial. When one of the chambers is at work a light glows in the lantern on the Capitol's dome and a flag is flown over that particular chamber.

Left: *the huge bronze of five marines and a sailor that forms the Marine Corps Memorial at Arlington National Cemetery.*

Above: *a military parade in Arlington National Cemetery passes the massive Marine Corps Memorial.*

Left: *the Marine Corps Memorial, depicting the raising of Old Glory on the Pacific island of Iwo Jima in 1945.*

*The Custis-Lee House in Arlington National Cemetery. This
southern mansion was once the home of the Robert E. Lee family
and much of the furniture, artwork and housewares on display to
the public here was actually used by the Lees.*

Below: *Arlington National Cemetery. Lying across the Virginia hills, just over the Arlington Memorial Bridge, this is a serene testament to the United States' military sacrifices – 1,100 acres of rolling hills dotted with simple headstones as far as the eye can see.*

The blood red leaves of fall hang over ranks of graves in Arlington National Cemetery, which is reserved for officers, enlistees and families of the military and the government. Famous politicians – even Presidents – as well as renowned soldiers are buried here.

Below: *a fall of snow emphasizes the stillness of Arlington National Cemetery, where the dead of every major American conflict rest. A Memorial Amphitheater is the site of services of remembrance.*

AN AMERICAN
SOLDIER
KNOWN BUT TO GOD

A soldier salutes the Tomb of the Unknowns, Arlington National Cemetery, which is protected by the Old Guard of the Third Infantry. The soldier moves twenty-one steps past the tomb, stops for twenty-one seconds and then returns: the army's highest salute.

Snow covers all in Arlington National Cemetery, where over 60,000 people have been buried. Since it is believed that space in this, the most prestigious cemetery in the country, will run out by the year 2000, the authorities have set strict requirements for interment.

The bronze statue of the most famous of American Freemasons that stands in the Memorial Hall of the George Washington Masonic National Memorial in Alexandria. It was unveiled by President Truman, another Freemason President, in 1950.

Above: *the arresting bronze of Simon Bolivar in a small park on 18th Street. Bolivar was the liberator of several South American republics and is revered today as the greatest Latin American hero. Ironically, when he died he was both poor and widely hated.*

The Einstein Memorial in the grounds of the National Academy of Sciences. The bronze figure sits before a "pool" of marble, relaxed and unassuming. Such a depiction of Einstein – always a humble man for all his scientific brilliance – seems quite appropriate.

Facing page: *the United States Army First Division Memorial, entitled "Victory" which stands in State Place near the Old Executive Office Building.*

Above: *the sculpture of Admiral Farragut which stands in Farragut Square. It was cast from the metal propeller of the U.S.S.* Hartford, *his flagship.*

Right: *the flaming sword of the U.S. Army Second Division First World War Memorial, which stands outside the Ellipse on Constitution Avenue.*

Above: *the Naval Observatory, where the Master Clock of the United States, the world's most accurate timepiece, is kept.*
Right: *the splendid interior of the Library of Congress.*

Washington's Magnificent Museums

For its first four decades, Washington was more concerned with survival than with culture. While public museums were opening in Philadelphia and New York, it was not until 1846, after ten years of debate, that Congress finally decided what to do with James Smithson's bequest, and the Smithsonian Institution was born. Even then, it was intended as a research facility, not a showcase for history or art. The first small beginnings in 1846 of what is now the Museum of American Art, and the private Corcoran Gallery, founded in 1869, were the only stirring of aesthetics in the capital.

In this century, however, Washington has more than made up for a slow start. Few cities in this or any country can match today's treasury of culture. And Smithson, an Englishman who had never visited America, would surely be amazed to see the complex of world class museums that have grown up under his name.

The Smithsonian Institution

This astounding organization oversees thirteen museums and the National Zoo, plus fourteen libraries, six research centers, including an Astrophysical Observatory, and the Cooper Hewitt Museum in New York. Together, these account for well over twenty-eight million visitors a year. In addition, the Kennedy Center, Woodrow Wilson

Above: *the entrance hall of the National Gallery of Art.*

International Center, and the National Gallery of Art are considered Smithsonian Institutions, even though they operate with independent boards and budgets.

The operating budget of this vast empire is over three hundred million dollars. Among the Smithsonian's holdings are some 135 million specimens, animals, artworks, and artifacts serving as a showcase of science, history, technology, art, and culture in America. The interests of the various museums extend to every phase of American life, and the collections range from fine art to George Washington's false teeth, prehistoric fossils to Muhammad Ali's boxing gloves. So rich are the possessions of the Smithsonian Museums that ninety-nine percent of them must be stored out of public view, explaining the nickname "the nation's attic."

Still a privately chartered body, the Smithsonian is governed by a Board of Regents whose chancellor is the chief justice of the United States. The regents include the president, vice president, and the heads of the executive departments, three senators, three members of the House of Representatives and nine private citizens.

James Smithson, the British scientist who began all of this, was the illegitimate son of the first Duke of Northumberland. In 1826, Smithson, a bachelor, willed what was then a considerable fortune, a cartload of gold sovereigns worth over half a million dollars, to the United States to create "at Washington, under the name of the Smithsonian Institution, an establishment for the increase and diffusion of knowledge among men." With prophetic foresight, Smithson added, "My name shall live in the memory of man when the titles of the Northumberlands and Percys are extinct."

In belated appreciation, the donor's body was brought to Washington in 1904, and his tomb installed in a place of honor just inside the Mall entrance, with exhibits about his life.

Congress accepted the bequest in 1835, but was slow to act on the generous gift. The Smithsonian was finally established in 1846 to conduct scientific research and to publish original findings. Today its realm reaches from ancient art to the frontiers of space.

The nine museums along the Mall offer both entertainment and enlightenment to the millions who visit Washington each year. When Mall space became scarce, the Smithsonian went underground with a research and education complex and two museums, all beneath the four-acre Enid A. Haupt Garden.

The tower of the Smithsonian Institution Building, popularly known as the "Castle," which stands on the Mall. The Institute administers thirteen museums and galleries in Washington. Just inside the entrance is the tomb of James Smithson, the English benefactor to whom the Smithsonian owes its existence.

"The Castle"

The first Smithsonian Institution Building, popularly known as "the castle," is red sandstone constructed in the style of a twelfth-century Norman revival castle. It was designed by James Renwick, Jr., the architect of New York's St. Patrick's Cathedral as well as the Renwick Gallery in Washington. The building originally contained laboratories and offices, a lecture hall, an art gallery, and a science museum. Scientists doing research there were offered living quarters in the tower.

The Institution's first secretary, Joseph Henry, moved his family into the second floor and carried on research concerning electricity and magnetism. Henry was also interested in weather and used balloons to collect data. When Samuel F.B. Morse demonstrated the first telegraph, Henry recognized its importance for weather forecasting and organized a network of 150 weather observers, who telegraphed weather data to the Smithsonian. When dangerous patterns were observed, officials flashed warning signals to coastal authorities from the tower. This was the inspiration for the United States Weather Bureau.

The castle was restored after a fire in 1865 and remodeled in the 1880s. Extensive renovations in the late 1980s created new functions for the old building including a Visitor Information Center and a reception center for Smithsonian Associates. The building also serves as a focus for the Woodrow Wilson International Center for Scholars.

National Air and Space Museum

The most popular of all the Smithsonian's museums is the National Air and Space Museum. The three-block-long glass and marble tribute to man's triumphs in flight was designed by architect Gyo Obata and opened on July 1, 1976, as part of the nation's Bicentennial Celebration.

There are some twenty-three acres of exhibits here, tracing the history of aviation in colorful fashion. Many aircraft hang overhead on wires as if in flight. In the "Milestones of Flight" gallery are treasures such as the *Langley Aerodrome #5*, designed by Samuel Langley, the third secretary of the Smithsonian, whose craft made a ninety-second unmanned flight in 1896. The Wright Brothers' craft in which Orville made the first manned flight at Kitty Hawk in 1903 is here, along with Charles Lindbergh's *Spirit of St. Louis*, the plane he flew in his historic solo journey across the Atlantic.

The U.S. Space Program is well represented with craft such as *Friendship 7*, in which John Glenn became the first American to orbit the earth in 1962, and the *Apollo II* command module *Columbia* that brought Neil Armstrong and his crew back from the

Right: *the Smithsonian "Castle," built in 1855 in the manner of a twelfth-century Italian Romanesque castle.*

Above: *small trees soften the rectangles of the John F. Kennedy Center for the Performing Arts.*

first moon landing. *Pioneer 10*, the first spacecraft to explore Jupiter, is also on display.

Exhibits here range from balloons to rockets to helicoptors, from the bright red Vega Amelia Earhart flew on the first solo transatlantic flight by a woman, to the *Skylab Orbital Workshop*, a model of America's first space station. Also part of the museum is the Albert Einstein Planetarium, an art gallery displaying artist's perceptions of air and space, and the Samuel P. Langley Theater, where films shown on a giant IMAX screen (five stories high and seven stories wide) give a realistic sense of the adventure of flight.

National Museum of American History

This is entertaining education at its best, actually a collection of museums tracing the social history, the everyday lives of Americans over two hundred years. Some sixteen million objects cover almost every conceivable phase of life – communication, transportation, agriculture, military uniforms, firearms, medicine, money, newspapers, musical instruments, stamps, coins, clocks, ceramics, computers, textiles, glass, and popular entertainment – to name a few.

It was known as the National Museum of History and Technology when it opened in 1964, in a building designed by McKim, Mead & White. In 1980, the present name was given, marking a change in emphasis to human history. The museum does not just show the advances in technology, but portrays how they affected peoples lives. The effects on the average family of inventions such as the railroad and automobile, the electric light and sewing machine are illustrated. Weaving to whaling, trusses to telephones, American ingenuity over the years is displayed here.

There are treasures here, as well, from gold coins to Tiffany lamps and Steuben glass. The effect of the earth's rotation is seen by watching the great Foucault Pendulum at the center of the building, and the infamous bare-breasted statue of George Washington, dressed as a Roman emperor, can be seen here. The original Star Spangled Banner, the flag that flew over Baltimore's Fort McHenry and inspired Francis Scott Key to write the national anthem, is in Flag Hall. To preserve the fabric, it is kept behind a curtain and lowered for two minutes every hour on the half hour.

Visitors are always intrigued by the First Ladies Hall, where the gowns worn at presidential inaugural balls over the years are displayed in period room settings. And everyone enjoys the entertainment section. Among its exhibits are the armchairs used on the set of "All in the Family," the ruby slippers Judy Garland wore in *The Wizard of Oz*, and the batons used by conductor Arturo Toscanini. The twentieth anniversary of the children's series "Sesame Street" and the one hundredth birthday of composer Irving Berlin were marked here.

National Museum of Natural History

The largest African elephant and Bengal tiger ever captured, a ninety-two-foot blue whale, dinosaurs, a giant woolly mammoth, and the famous Hope Diamond, at 45.5 carats, the largest blue diamond in the world – all of these wonders can be found at the National Museum of Natural History, a favorite since it opened in 1910.

Starring in the four-story pillared and domed rotunda is one of the largest animals in the world, an African bull elephant weighing eight tons and standing thirteen feet tall. In galleries adjoining are some of the most spectacular dinosaur finds. There are galleries for birds, fish, reptiles, and mammals. Not forgotten is our own species. The recreation of a burial of a young Neanderthal man in a French cave seventy thousand years ago; halls of Eskimo, Indian, Pacific, African, and South American cultures; and a huge stone head from Easter Island are all part of the story of man.

Meteorites, minerals, and moon rocks are also displayed. The Hall of Gems holds special fascination, with over one thousand precious and semi-precious stones. Besides the Hope Diamond, there is the 330-carat Star of Asia, one of the world's great star sapphires. Other baubles include a 127-carat Portugese diamond, the 138.7-carat Rosser Reeves ruby (the largest ruby in the world), a 423-carat sapphire, and the 31-carat heart-shaped Eugenie blue diamond – not to mention Marie-Antoinette's 950-carat diamond tiara, and the diamond necklace Napoleon I gave to his wife, Marie Louise. Also displayed is what one guide calls "all the jade in China."

One of the favorite exhibits of this museum stands outside the door. It is "Uncle Beazley," the life-size model of a triceratops dinosaur who holds court on the Mall, a favorite climbing surface for generations of children visiting the capital.

Arts and Industries Building

Originally known as the National Museum, this brick and sandstone structure is the Smithsonian's second oldest, dating to 1881. It was created to hold the exhibits from the American Centennial Exposition in Philadelphia in 1876. A ten-year restoration beginning in 1976 recreated the style of the original exhibition, retaining the aura of Victorian times. A skylit rotunda with a fountain and fresh flowers is at the center of the cross-shaped building, leading to four wings crammed with exhibits. This is museum-going the way it used to be, a building filled with curiosities

and dusty corners. All the contents were either shown at the Exposition or made during that period.

Beside household items and industrial exhibits of the period, there are the exhibits sent to the Centennial exposition by other countries – silks from Siam, porcelain from Japan and Russia, furniture from China – and displays set up by each state representing their histories and industries. Upstairs, the Horticultural Hall is also a recreation of the 1876 original, an extravanganza filled with the ferns and exotic plants that decorated Victorian interiors.

Hirshhorn Museum and Sculpture Garden

The Smithsonian's museum of modern and contemporary art was the 1966 gift of a private collector, Joseph Hirshhorn, a man who rose from New York's slums to make a fortune in finance and uranium mines. For more than thirty years, Hirshhorn was on a perennial art-buying spree. His total collection numbered more than thirteen thousand works. Critics called him a human vacuum cleaner, but while some of his art choices were uneven, he also culled treasures. Among the artists represented are Eakins, Sargent, Rodin, Degas, Moore, Daumier, Matisse, Calder, Picasso, Giacometti, Miro, de Kooning, Gorky, and David Smith. He was especially fond of the work of American painter Thomas Eakins, and owned more than fifty of his canvasses.

The boy who never had a toy grew into a man with a special love for things he could touch, and Hirshhorn's sculptures were his pride and most important contribution to the art world. They filled his lawns and his warehouses; even a museum cannot hold them all. He gave the nation more than two thousand sculptures.

The modernistic building Hirshhorn donated to hold his works was the most controversial structure on the Mall when it opened in 1974. It has been dubbed a floating bunker and a donut. It is actually an eight-story cylinder designed by architect Gordon Bunshaft with a three-acre plaza to display monumental sculpture and a garden holding another seventy-five pieces on a more intimate scale. Among the prizes to be seen here are *The Burghers of Calais*, an 1886 bronze by Rodin; a corner devoted to whimsical works by David Smith; and sculptures by Henry Moore and Alexander Calder.

Freer Gallery of Art

The Freer is an unsung gem among the Smithsonian museums, a delightful surprise to many art lovers. Behind the elegant Renaissance facade of this gallery are the collections of Detroit industrialist Charles Lang Freer, another self-made millionaire who

The Kennedy Center, situated beside the Potomac River, is one of the country's most prestigious platforms for performing artistes.

founded the Peninsular Car Works, the first factory to manufacture railroad cars in the Midwest. His donations included the largest collection of works by James McNeill Whistler in North America, including Whistler's noted Peacock Room, designed for a London town house, as well as a vast and priceless collection of Oriental art. The riches include over one thousand works by Whistler and more than ten thousand objects of Chinese, Japanese, Indian, Korean, Tibetan, and Middle Eastern art. Prize among the holdings are Chinese bronze, ceramica, and porcelain, and one of the finest Islamic painting collections in North America.

Freer, a bachelor, wrote to Theodore Roosevelt in 1903 offering his art collection to the nation on his death. It was the first significant art to be donated to the government. A committee headed by Alexander Graham Bell went to Detroit to decide the worthiness of the collection. By then it had become so enormous that the inspection took five days.

Freer also offered funds for a new building to house the collection after his death, but with the stipulation that nothing could be added or loaned out. He selected Charles A. Platt of New York as architect and worked closely with him on the design, which is built around a central courtyard garden, a plan resembling a Florentine Renaissance palace. It opened to the public in the spring of 1921. The museum is connected by an underground passage to a second showcase for Asian art, the Sackler Gallery, which opened in 1987. A major renovation began at the Freer in 1988.

The Quadrangle

The Arthur M. Sackler Gallery, along with the Museum of African Art and the S. Dillon Ripley International Center, was constructed underneath the splendid four-acre Enid A. Haupt Garden. The museums, though primarily below ground, are topped with striking rooflines that reflect the art inside and have good ground-level entrances with stairs leading to the exhibits.

Arthur Sackler was a medical researcher and publisher who made his fortune from the development of the tranquilizing drug Valium. His fine collection,

one thousand works of Asian and Near Eastern art, augments and extends the Freer. The two museums share a staff, a library, and conservation lab. Unlike the Freer, this newer museum welcomes borrowed shows, and will lend from its collections.

Among the valuable Sackler items are 475 Chinese jades dating from the Neolithic era, 5000 to 1500 B.C., to the twentieth century; gold and silver treasures; illuminated Persian manuscripts; 153 Chinese bronzes from the Sang through Han dynasties; 68 Chinese paintings from the tenth to the twentieth centuries; and 48 choice examples of Chinese laquerware. The museum also houses the Vever collection, one of the world's most distinguished collections of ancient Persian art, which was purchased by the Smithsonian for seven million dollars in 1986.

Another equally fascinating museum is the National Museum of African Art, which stands as the Smithsonian's recognition of the increasing need for an understanding of non-Western cultures. The museum holds two permanent African collections of some 8,000 pieces and all the exhibits are labelled in English and Swahili. Much of the focus is on sub-Saharan Africa, and the visitor will find not only exhibition galleries but also a library and photographic archives devoted to the continent.

This art did not come from a patron of great

Above: abstract bronzes complement the National Gallery's East Building.

Facing page: marble statues of cherubic children in the National Gallery of Art.

wealth. It was the private museum of Warren Roberts, who was a school teacher in New Hampshire and later cultural attache in Germany and Austria. The collection was formerly housed in a row of houses in Washington dedicated to showing works by African-Americans. The collection was absorbed by the Smithsonian in 1979 and opened in its handsome new quarters in 1987. Excellent loan collections of African art are also shown here.

The final underground structure, the S. Dillion Ripley Center, is named for a past director of the Smithsonian. It houses a major exhibition gallery and offers films and lectures approaching art from a non-western perspective.

The National Gallery of Art

Perhaps the most prestigious of all Washington's museums is the National Gallery. Some seven million people visit each year, outdrawing even New York's older and much larger Metropolitan Museum. It is Washington's Louvre and Museum of Modern Art rolled into one.

The museum was actually born in the 1920s when

millionaire industrialist and Treasury Secretary Andrew W. Mellon decided to build an art collection that would eventually form the nucleus of a National Gallery. In 1937 Congress made it official. The Mellon Trust donated funds for construction of the building and the salaries of its executives, and the museum opened in 1941 with 121 paintings donated by Mellon. These included important works Mellon acquired after the Russian Revolution, when the Russians were running out of cash and put works of art from the Hermitage Museum in Leningrad on sale. Among these were works by Botticelli, Raphael, Titian, Rembrandt, Van Dyck, and Hals.

Today the National Gallery consists of two buildings spanning the history of Western art and contains many more masterpieces, including the only Leonardo da Vinci found outside Europe. The original West Building designed by John Russell Pope, the architect of the Jefferson Memorial, was built on a monumental scale. It is one of the world's largest marble structures with more than five hundred thousand square feet of interior space, adorned with lofty marble columns and fountains. The masterpieces in this building trace the full development of Western art from da Vinci to Picasso.

The East Building architect, I.M. Pei, faced the challenge of blending the original building with a modern addition that was set on a trapezoidal site. His brilliant solution was to divide the building into two interlocking triangles, a study in symmetry that somehow works with its neo-classical neighbor. The vast and airy building, which was funded by the Mellon Foundation, is designed with open balconies and bridges and filled with green plants and cafes, which almost give the feel of an indoor park. When it opened in 1978, it nearly doubled the museum's space. Besides housing the permanent twentieth-century collections, which include Picasso, Matisse, Rothko,

The Small Museum Gems

Many of Washington's art treasures are its smaller, lesser-known collections that are equally notable for their elegant surroundings.

The Corcoran Gallery of Art was Washington's first museum, founded in 1859, and it is still one of the finest places in the nation to see American art. Originally housed in the building now known as the Renwick Gallery, it moved in 1897 to its present fine marble Beaux Arts home, a building designed by

Facing page: *the roof of I.M. Pei's East Building of the National Gallery of Art. This Seventies design uses the same marble as the main Gallery.*

Above: *the famous Calder mobile, one of the world's largest and typical of the modern art in the East Building of the National Gallery.*

Right: *the sheer tower of the National Gallery's angular East Building, which edges Pennsylvania Avenue within sight of the Capitol.*

Facing page: *a recumbent stone lion welcomes visitors to the Corcoran Gallery, one of the oldest art museums in the country.*

Above: *the marble Beaux-Arts-style building by Ernest Flagg that houses the Corcoran Gallery. The gallery was founded in 1859.*

Ernest Flagg with beautifully proportioned high ceilings and skylit galleries that add to the pleasure of a visit. Frank Lloyd Wright called it "the best designed building in Washington."

The museum was first dedicated to American genius. Its paintings include work by Copley, Stuart, Rembrandt, Peale, Church, Sargent, Eakins, and Homer, much of it acquired by founder William Wilson Corcoran, founder of the Riggs Bank in Washington. Corcoran also began the collection of photographs, which has been continued for more than one hundred years.

The American works were augmented in 1925 by the donation of Senator William A. Clark's collection of European art, and the late nineteenth and twentieth-century paintings of Mr. and Mrs. Edward Walter.

The Renwick Gallery was completed in 1874 to house the original Corcoran Gallery. The grand design was in Second Empire style with a curved mansard roof. Inside a large stairway ascends from the first floor to a ninety-foot-long Grand Salon and an Octagonal Room. When the Corcoran outgrew the space, the building served a variety of uses and was in a state of deterioration until it was turned over to the Smithsonian in 1965. The elegant original interior was carefully restored and the building reopened in 1972 as a gallery of arts, crafts, and design.

The oldest of the federal collections, the National Museum of American Art, is another underrated showplace dedicated to American art. It also started with one man, John Varden, who began collecting as early as 1829 and advertised his "Washington Museum" in 1836. The Varden collection was incorporated into the newly founded National Institute in 1841, and an exhibition space was established in the Patent Office Building, a venerable Washington structure whose porticoes are said to be exact reproductions of the Parthenon in Athens. The displays here included paintings, sculpture, and historic documents.

The museum was known as the National Gallery until the Mellon Gallery was created. It was then renamed the National Collection of Fine Arts. The present more accurate name was given in 1980. The collection is an overview of American art from colonial times to the present, some thirty-two thousand works from Charles Willson Peale to Andrew Wyeth.

The National Portrait Gallery, established by Congress in 1971, occupies the other half of the old

Patent Office Building. It is an imposing showcase for rows of paintings of distinguished citizens. All the presidents can be seen, along with artists, poets, entertainers, musicians and sports figures. Davy Crockett, Thomas Edison, John D. Rockefeller, Phineas T. Barnum, Helen Keller, Martin Luther King, Babe Ruth, Walt Disney, and Will Rogers are among those immortalized here. Some of the best of the eight thousand portraits are photographs, including Alexander Gardner's photo of Lincoln taken four days before the president was shot.

The Phillips Collection was the first American museum for modern art. Founder Duncan Phillips, the grandson of the founder of the Jones and Laughlin Steel Company, began collecting soon after his graduation from Lale in 1908. The museum was founded in memory of his recently deceased father and brother in 1921. It has grown from 240 to 2,500 paintings. The most important are French Impressionists, Post-Impressionists, and American Modernists. They are shown in the warm, home-like setting of an 1897 Georgian Revival brownstone, in rooms filled with Oriental rugs and fine furnishings as well as beautiful art.

The National Museum of Women in the Arts opened in 1987 in a lavishly refurbished Masonic lodge, resplendent with crystal chandeliers, sweeping marble stairs, walls of silk, and floral decorations in gold leaf. Founder Wilhelmina Cole Holladay planned this museum to pay tribute to overlooked women painters. She had raised sixteen million dollars to support her cause even before the museum opened its doors. Among those represented are Mary Cassatt, Georgia O'Keefe, Alice Neel, Lee Krasner, and many female painters whose names are less well known, dating all the way back to 1580.

There are dozens of other collections throughout Washington, something for every taste and interest. The Textile Museum, housed in two elegant old homes with a garden in back, boasts exhibits from ancient Peruvian fabrics to Persian carpets, some eighty-five-hundred textiles and eight hundred rugs in all. It was founded by George Hewitt Myers of Bristol Myers in 1925; he lived in one of the homes until he died in 1957.

The D.A.R. Museum can be found in the Memorial Continental Hall. Here, over thirty rooms have been decorated and furnished by individual states to show how life was lived in America since colonial times. The Oklahoma Room is a prairie farm kitchen, for example, while the Missouri Room has become a steamboat parlor.

An extraordinary collection of pre-Renaissance European art – plus one of the city's most beautiful

The imposing Memorial Constitution Hall.

Above: *Dumbarton Oaks, home to a collection of Byzantine art.*

formal gardens – is at the Dumbarton Oaks Byzantine and Pre-Columbian Collections in Georgetown. Again, this was the home of an individual family, Mr. and Mrs. Robert Woods Bliss, who filled it with their art and in 1940 gave it all to Harvard University. It is now a research center for the study of Byzantine medieval history and culture as well as a museum.

Literary Washington

In this city dedicated to "We, the People," there is truly something for everyone – including those whose tastes are literary.

The world's largest collection of the plays and poetry of William Shakespeare is not at Stratford-on-Avon, but in Washington, D.C., at the Folger Shakespeare Library. It all began in 1879 when Henry Clay Folger, inspired by a lecture given by Ralph Waldo Emerson at Amherst College, purchased a small edition of Shakespeare's work. As he progressed to chairman of the board of the Standard Oil Company of New York, Folger was able to acquire an unparalleled library.

After considering locations in both England and America, patriotism coupled with Mrs. Folger's fondness for her childhood home in Washington led them to select a site on Capitol Hill for a research library to house his volumes. There are some 280,000 books and manuscripts, nearly 100,000 of them considered rare. The Library also sponsors seminars, lectures, and concerts. The big event of the year is the celebration of Shakespeare's birthday on April 23, with music, entertainment, and guided tours of the Elizabethan garden and the rare book vaults.

A treasury of Americana awaits at the National Archives, the place to see the original documents that

Sunset lights up the Bureau of Engraving and Printing.

guided our country's destiny – the Declaration of Independence, the Constitution, and the Bill of Rights. Also inside this sanctum adorned with murals of the founding fathers are the journals of the Continental Congress, Washington's letter reporting the victory at Yorktown, and the Treaty of Paris that ended the American Revolution. The huge archives may be used as a library for anyone researching early census, pension, or military records or researching family history.

No library equals the Library of Congress, the largest library in the world. There are over 500 miles of shelves holding more than eighty-four million items. It has been estimated that some 35,000 new items come in every week.

When the original library in the Capitol building was burned by the British, Thomas Jefferson sold his large personal library to give the institution a new start. The 6,487 books, many of them rare, were purchased for $23,950. Today every book published in the United States must be deposited here for copyright. And every single one is available to the public. All it takes is filling out a request slip.

There are also countless foreign publications,

Left: *the ceiling of the Library of Congress, which wouldn't disgrace an opera house. Upon completion in 1897, the building was the most expensive in the world.*

Right: *a bronze of a wild horse and its naked rider – a subject typical of the late nineteenth century – in the environs of the Library of Congress.*

Below: *students studying in the Main Reading Room of the Library of Congress, an ornate Beaux-Arts building designed after the Paris Opera House.*

including such rarities as a fifteenth-century copy of the Book of Psalms in Hebrew and the world's first printed encyclopedia, 5,040 volumes in Chinese.

The library finally got its own home in 1897, an Italian Renaissance showplace of New Hampshire granite with fifteen kinds of marble gracing the interior. Fifty American artists and twenty sculptors embellished the building with words devoted to the themes of knowledge and learning. In the main reading rooms are works by Daniel Chester French and Augustus Saint-Gaudens, the leading sculptors of their day.

There are exhibits of rare books in the magnificent pillared Great Hall, where a Gutenberg Bible and the Giant Bible of Mainz are the prize displays. Also displayed in other locations are the year's best news photographs, and special exhibits that may vary from a history of Disney animation to a survey of cowboy art. The library has been extended twice, with the additions of the John Adams Building in 1939 and the James Madison Memorial Building in 1980. The three buildings are connected by underground tunnels.

Chamber music concerts, lectures, and poetry readings are also on the agenda of this truly remarkable Washington institution.

Above: *tourists relax in one of Washington's many parks.*
Right: *Georgetown residences, today considered to be some of the most desirable in the capital.*

The People's Washington

Stately columns, museums, and statues make for handsome vistas, but they are not what makes the heart of a city. For the nearly 650,000 who live in the District of Columbia and the total of over three million in the metropolitan area, official Washington takes second place to their own Washington, a livable city of neighborhoods filled with pockets of color and charm. In these neighborhoods live not only politicians and diplomats, but everyday people from every walk of life. They have many interests beyond what happens on Capitol Hill – such as gardening, babysitters, where to eat on Saturday night, and far from least, the fortunes of their beloved football team, the Redskins. On a football weekend, vendors with pennants and buttons make the street corners of the capital resemble a stadium.

Washingtonians never tire of exploring their own city, and there is plenty to keep them occupied. There are reportedly ninety-five recognized neighborhoods over the sixty-three square miles of the District of Columbia. Twenty of them have been named historic districts, significant for their architecture and place in the city's history.

This is also a city made to order for outdoor lovers. It is rich in parks and playgrounds.

Getting from one place to another is easy since the city installed its model Metrorail system, a sleek, speedy, silent, and spotless underground network that covers 1,489 square miles in D.C. and nearby Maryland and Virginia, efficiently handling almost a million trips a day.

Above: *a working gas lamp outside a Georgetown door.*

Left: *Georgetown University in winter, framed by an arch of the Francis Scott Key Bridge.*

Right: *the Georgetown women's rowing crew pass under Arlington Memorial Bridge on the Potomac River.*

Above: *a red umbrella brightens a monochrome snowscape in the environs of Georgetown University.*

LIVE-IN WASHINGTON: THE NEIGHBORHOODS

Georgetown

The best-known neighborhood in the city is also the oldest. Georgetown was a busy port before there ever was a Washington. Named for the reigning King, George II, it was incorporated with its own mayor in 1742. Tobacco was the gold that made Georgetown's traders rich. Barrels of the precious stuff were loaded aboard clipper ships bound for faraway lands.

Though only a few of the earliest eighteenth-century buildings remain, the streets uphill north of M Street are treasures, cobbled lanes lined with towering trees and fine homes built in the nineteenth century. John F. Kennedy lived here; so did Robert Todd Lincoln and Francis Scott Key.

127

Georgetown began to lose its luster as the clipper trade lost out to steamships and railroads. By the time it became part of the District of Columbia in 1871, it was looking decidedly down at the heels. Then in the 1930s and 1940s it was rediscovered. Official Washington began moving in, and restoring a historic house was soon the thing to do in society and political circles. Real estate values began to spiral and when the area was named a National Historic District in 1967, things got really out of hand.

A stroll through the neighborhood leads past some fascinating history. The Old Stone House is believed to be the oldest surviving pre-revolutionary building in Georgetown. The house is open to the public, as is its garden, a pleasant oasis in the city. Another of the oldest late-Georgian homes, the 1747 Dumbarton House, has become the headquarters of the National Society of the Colonial Dames of America.

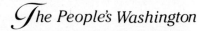

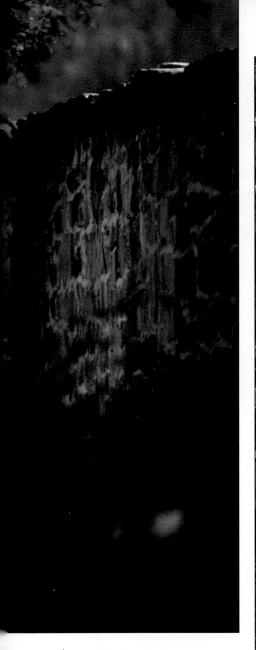

Above: *Georgetown residents stroll along a lane that, in its relaxed charm, is typical of this beautiful Washington suburb.*

Left: *painted brickwork, polished house numbers and a sycamore in the fall – quintessential Georgetown.*

Right: *the Glenwood area, Northwest Washington. Square miles of these row houses were constructed in the 1870s.*

Above: Georgetown shopfronts reflect the exclusivity of this, the most affluent and select of Washington suburbs.

Right: a residential street in Georgetown, where Victorian and Federal architecture is lovingly preserved.

Left: tramlines bisect a fall avenue in Georgetown. In Washington it is often better to leave the car and take the bus.

Other historic houses include the 1799 Laird-Dunlop House, the three-story home of tobacco trader John Laird, which was later occupied by James Dunlop, a chief justice of the Supreme Court, and from 1915 to 1926 by Robert Todd Lincoln, the president's son, who served as secretary of war and ambassador to England. The nearby 1794 Beall House was built by Thomas Beall, the mayor of Georgetown, who met with George Washington here to discuss the town's incorporation into the district. Jacqueline Kennedy lived here following her husband's assassination. The Kennedy family lived in a red brick home on N Street, which the senator bought for his wife after the birth of their daughter, Caroline.

Evermay, a two-story Georgian mansion with an Italian terraced garden and gurgling fountain, was built on a site acquired by Samuel Davidson in 1794, after he sold to the government the land where the

131

White House and Lafayette Park now stand.

The great Dumbarton Oaks estate, mentioned earlier, was built around 1800; John C. Calhoun lived here when he served in the Senate. The ten-acre gardens are a special delight, offering some one thousand roses, fountains, and the best of Italian, English, and French garden design.

Georgetown's churches have also seen their share of history. Francis Scott Key, the author of "The Star Spangled Banner," was an active member of St. John's Church, along with many other well-known Washington residents. Abraham Lincoln was said to have wept during a wartime service at the Methodist Episcopal Church. It later served as a Union hospital where Walt Whitman was one of the volunteers caring for the wounded.

Above: *iron railings, floor-to-ceiling sash windows and a grand piano betoken an elegant Georgetown residence.*

Right: *part of the extensive gardens at Dumbarton Oaks, which include a rose garden boasting 1,000 roses.*

Above: *a Georgetown University crew rows past the Lincoln Memorial at dawn, when river traffic is light.*

Left: *Georgetown University's founder, John Carroll, who was America's first Catholic bishop.*

Another historic resident of the neighborhood is Georgetown University, the oldest Catholic School in the United States. It was founded by Bishop John Carroll in 1789 and was the first university in the country to train students for international business and the diplomatic service at its renowned school of Foreign Service.

Wisconsin Avenue and M Street are the commercial hearts of Georgetown, referred to locally as "The Strip." They are crammed with shops, restaurants, and clubs, including many of the city's favorite nightspots.

Georgetown University medical students leaving Medical School. During the Civil War, the Army Medical Corps took over some of the university's facilities for the care of the wounded.

Georgetown is also the starting point of George Washington's C & O Canal, which extends north along the Potomac for 185 miles. Intended to link the port to the Ohio River and the Atlantic Ocean, the canal was begun in 1828, but by the time the difficult project was completed in 1850, it had already been made almost obsolete by the coming of the railroad. Today the National Park Service offers summertime mule-drawn barge rides along the canal, a cooling pastime on a warm summer day.

One of the newest developments in the neighborhood, Washington Harbour, went up in 1986. The multi-use residential, office, and shopping complex provides a lovely courtyard and walkways with superb views of the river. The condominiums here, with gold bathroom fixtures and marble fireplaces, sell for upwards of two million dollars.

Above: *Washington Harbor, a residential, shopping and office complex constructed in 1986 beside the Potomac.*

Left: *Washington Harbor at night. This complex has become one of the most prestigious in the capital.*

Right: *the intricate architecture of the condominiums of Washington Harbor, typical of building design in the Eighties.*

Capitol Hill

Another lively section of the city is Capitol Hill. In the very shadow of the U.S. Capitol building are shady residential streets, a mix of Federal and Victorian brown houses, art galleries, sidewalk cafés and an old-style farmers' market. Senators and representatives live in this eclectic corner of the city, along with people from every walk of life.

In the early part of the century, Capitol Hill was a place of grand town houses, some of them mammoth brick castles with towers and balconies. When the wealthy began to migrate back to the suburbs, many of the old houses became tourist homes or apartments. Now families are beginning to reconvert some of the mansions. Some of the attractions are obvious; their neighborhood library, for example, is the Library of Congress. Those who took a chance on the neighborhood early made prudent investments.

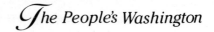

Above: *the nineteenth-century row houses of Capitol Hill, one of the oldest residential areas in Washington.*

Left: *Capitol Hill at night. Many Congressmen, Senators and other government and military figures live on the Hill.*

Right: *the tower of a Victorian Capitol Hill row house. The addition of a tower to a house was a popular Victorian touch.*

Eastern Market, built in 1871, is still a functioning centerpiece of the area and just the place to find fresh-picked produce, cut flowers, or a dozen farm-fresh eggs. It is packed on Friday and Saturday and in December when it is filled with Christmas greens. The donuts at the bakery are legendary.

A few blocks from the Capitol, Washington's Union Station has been reborn. The Amtrak train station here now shares space with a lively mix of one hundred shops, twenty-five restaurants and eating establishments, and a nine-screen movie theater. It has become a magnet for visitors as well as a meeting place for off-duty Washingtonians. Some forty thousand people now pass through the station daily.

The grand white granite Beaux Arts station, which opened in 1907 at a cost of $25 million, re-opened in 1988 after a $160 million restoration designed to preserve it as a national treasure. This was the largest, most complex public-private restoration project ever attempted in this country.

Dupont Circle, Kalorama, and Embassy Row

The streets leading into Dupont Circle, where New Hampshire, Massachusetts, and Connecticut Avenues converge, were "the" place to live in Washington from

Above: the Beaux-Arts front of the old Union Station, designed by Daniel Burnham in 1908. This monument to the railroads was built of granite. Its exterior is based on the Arch of Constantine in Rome.

Facing page: full of light, air and classical references, Union Station has been transformed. Today this elegant interior contains over 100 shops and a nine-screen cinema, as well as an Amtrack station.

Patrons of the Seasons Cafe, one of twenty-five places to eat in Union Station, are overlooked by classical statues designed to resemble the sculpture at the Baths of Diocletian in Rome.

the late 1800s well into the twentieth century. They remain fashionable, filled with art galleries, elegant Victorian row houses, and shops. Dupont Circle also is home to the Phillips Collection, the Textile Museum, and many other museums, as well as the house-museum of former President Woodrow Wilson.

Most of the city's 150 foreign embassies are found in the magnificent Victorian mansions extending west of Dupont Circle along Massachusetts Avenue, between Sheridan and Observatory Circles. They are a fine sight, resplendent with coats of arms and diplomatic flags. Among the handsome homes is the vice president's residence at Observatory Circle.

Adjacent Kalorama Road has some of the capital's loveliest homes

The atmosphere in Dupont Circle is far from rarefied. On the cross streets are blocks of row houses popular with government workers who can walk to their jobs. On weekends, the streets are full of browsers. There are impromptu concerts in the park and serious games of chess at the sidewalk game tables. The Circle, the hub of the neighborhood, is the place for people-watching.

In the 1960s, Dupont Circle was a gathering place for the hippies of that generation and the site of anti-war demonstrations. It is still a place where

Above: *the fountain that forms the centerpiece of Dupont Circle, sculpted by Daniel Chester French in 1921.*

Left: *Massachusetts Avenue terminates in Dupont Circle, a memorial to Rear Admiral du Pont, a Union naval hero.*

Right: *Old Glory and the Union Jack fly side by side outside Burberrys, a select English clothes store on Dupont Circle.*

demonstrators often mass, heading for the White House or the embassies nearby.

Adams Morgan

The area along Columbia between Eighteenth Street and Kalorama Park is known as Washington's "United Nations," an area where Washingtonians love to dine, to browse on weekends, and to join the annual festivals that turn the streets into a huge outdoor party and crafts display.

There is a strong Hispanic-Latin flavor to this multi-ethnic neighborhood, but one hundred or so

restaurants and cafes serve foods from around the world, South America to Japan to Ethiopia. Ethnic grocery stores, street vendors, antiques shops and galleries, and a Saturday flea market and flower stand add flavor and texture to the mix.

Downtown

Downtown Washington dates to the founding of the city in 1800, when it was both commercial and residential center of the new capital. It extends north of Pennsylvania Avenue, between the White House and Capitol. In early days many congressmen lived in rooming houses and hotels in the area and walked to work. Hotels remain, but the department stores, restaurants, offices, and the city's convention center have left little room for residences.

Pennsylvania Avenue, the nation's best-known address, has had a renaissance in recent years beyond the White House, with the restoration of landmarks such as the historic Willard Hotel and the Old Post Office, which has bloomed anew as a three-story shopping and dining complex. The historic 1899 building is the capital's oldest federal building

Above: *a cash point serves the public on Dupont Circle – here, as in any great Western capital, the credit card will provide.*

Left: *the magnificent gates of Chinatown. Such pockets of cultural pride flourish throughout Washington.*

Right: *a successful company's premises in Washington Square on K Street near Foggy Bottom, western downtown Washington.*

and second tallest structure. Visitors can ride a glass elevator up to the historic Clock Tower to take in a bird's-eye view of the city.

F Street Plaza is the downtown shopping hub, home to such long-established department stores as Woodward & Lothrop and Hecht's, as well as the newer centers such as the Shops at National Place and the Shops at the National Press Building.

The business lifeline of the city is K Street and the surrounding blocks running from Twelfth to Twenty-first Streets, N.W. Commerce is often livened here with lunchtime performances by street musicians.

Much of downtown from Fifteenth Street eastward is being revitalized. One example is the Franklin Park area surrounding Fourteenth Street, N.W. Until recently, it was a seedy red-light district. Now blocks of new buildings, restaurants, and shops have taken the place of the former "businesses."

The new Friendship Archway in Chinatown has paved the way for the renovation of that neighborhood also, an eight-square-block area surrounding H Street, N.W., between Sixth and Seventh Streets. Chinese-style street lamps and new restaurants are helping to revitalize the area's colorful character.

Old Anacostia

Named for its original Indian settlers, the neighborhood stretching across the Anacostia River from downtown dates to the arrival of John Smith in 1607 and has a unique place in city history. It was the original Washington settlement site for blacks after the Civil War.

Originally known as Washington County, the area grew up slowly and did not become an official part of the District until 1871, the same year Georgetown was taken in. In the 1850s, it was considered a place to escape city congestion. Many of the detached frame houses from that period stand clustered around the hilltop home of abolitionist Frederick Douglass. The Douglass house is an historic site maintained by the National Park Service. The Anacostia Neighborhood Museum offers exhibits on black history and culture.

The top of Morris Road in Anacostia provides one of the best panoramic views of the city.

Outdoor Washington

A city of bikers, joggers, and sailors, Washington's generally mild climate and riverside location make it perfect for outdoor activity. Few metropolitan areas offer so many escapes from city pavements. Washingtonians can paddle a boat, fish, horseback ride, windsurf, hike, or row without ever leaving town. Newcomers are happily surprised to note seagulls in downtown parks.

The National Capital Park Service, a division of the National Park Service, oversees most of the parkland, along with the city's monuments and memorials. Rock Creek Park, in the northwestern part of town adjacent to Georgetown, is a cool green 1,754-acre complex

Above: *the banks of the Potomac River serve as the seaside for Washingtonians relaxing at the weekend.*

Left: *Japanese cherry trees – the pride of the capital – blossom for lovers and loners alike beside the Tidal Basin.*

Right: *a tangle of bicycles outside Georgetown University. Students are among many who use bikes to beat the jams.*

Above: *afternoon sun highlights the Francis Scott Key Bridge, the Lincoln Memorial and the Washington Monument.*

Left: *the National Defense University which overlooks the confluence of the Potomac and Anacostia rivers.*

Right: *a fisherman casts his line in undisturbed peace on the Potomac River early on a summer's morning.*

providing many kinds of recreation – fifteen miles of hiking trails, two nine-hole golf courses, a jogging trail with eighteen par-course exercise stations, twenty-two tennis courts, horseback riding, and some thirty picnic areas. Far from the least of the park's attractions is the National Zoo. The stars here are Ling Ling and Hsing Hsing, the pair of giant pandas given by the Chinese government. Few matters in this political city provide such unified agreement as the desire to see the pair succeed in producing offspring. Besides the pandas, there are over two thousand other species to be visited.

Walkers and bikers enjoy the paths along the Chesapeake and Ohio Canal Park, particularly the grassy venues on the Maryland side of the Potomac at Great Falls. Huge craggy rocks line the river here, providing vistas of great beauty, and the bottomlands off the towpath are rich in wildflowers. In the rare

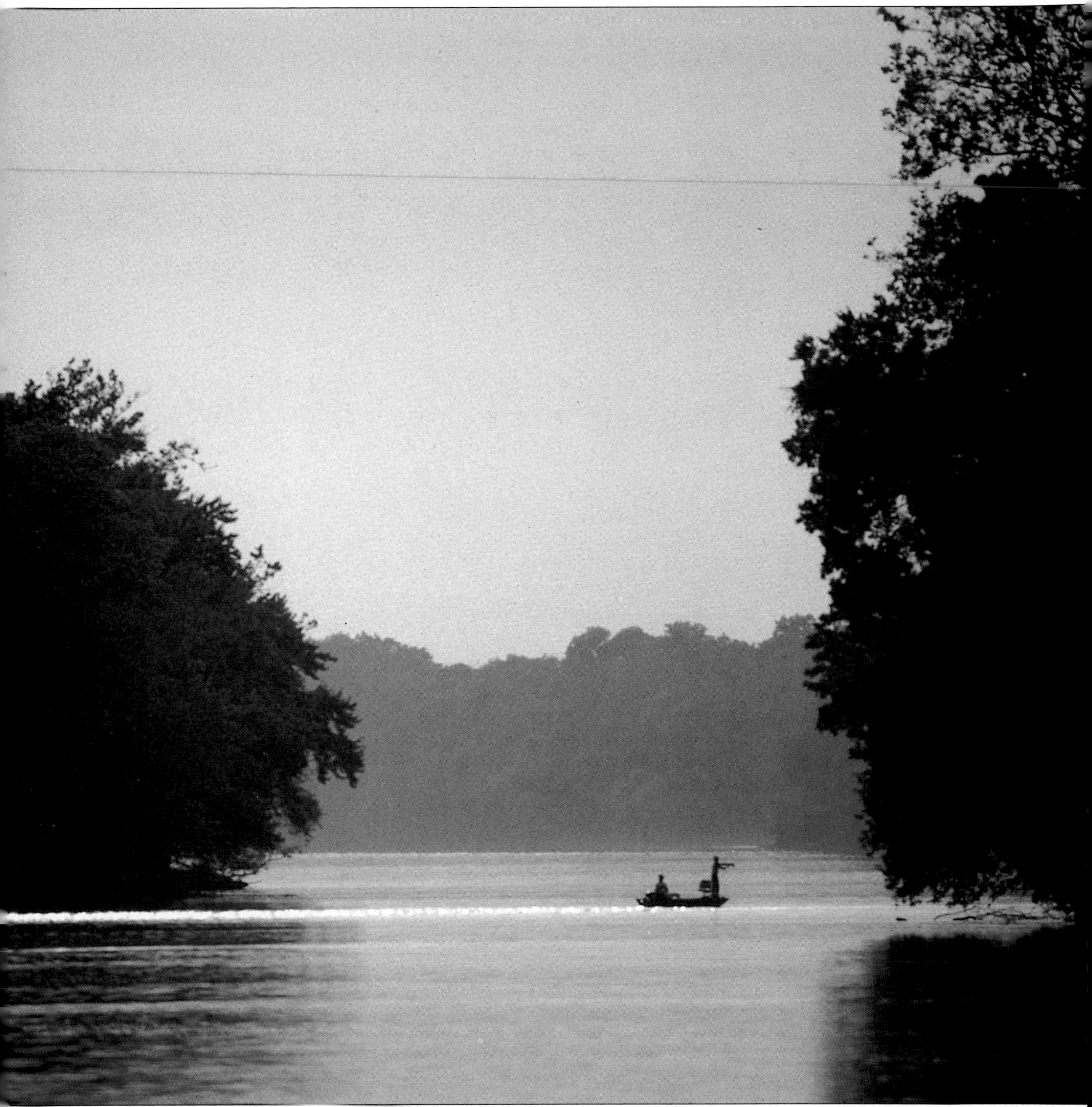

Left: *two sisters pose under the cherry blossom that surrounds the Tidal Basin in spring.*

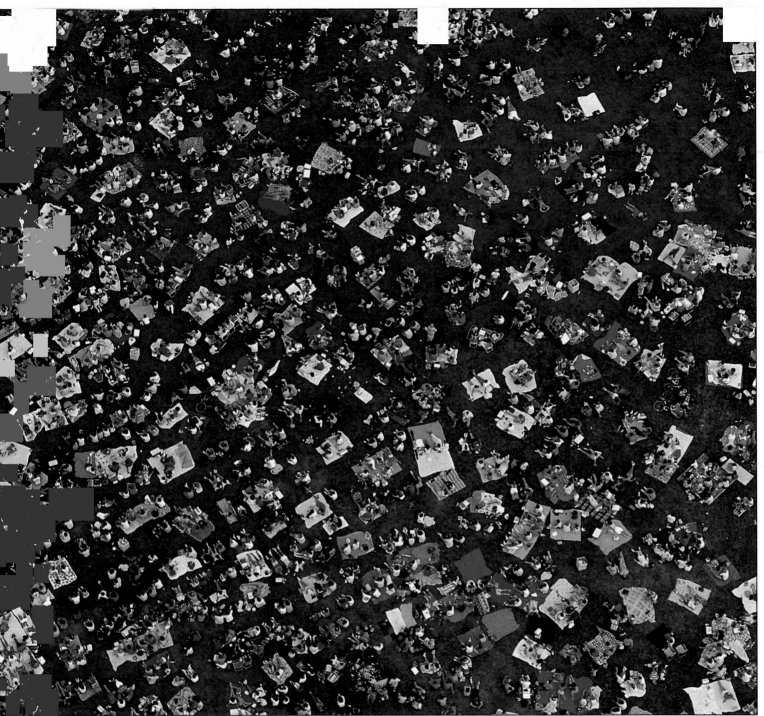

Crowds gather for the July 4 celebrations in the grounds of the Washington Monument. The festivities include speeches, singers, military bands and a spectacular display of fireworks.

winters when freezing occurs, city residents gleefully enjoy skating on sections of the frozen canal.

Theodore Roosevelt Island off the George Washington Memorial Parkway is another welcome escape not far from downtown, a deeply wooded isle that is a wildlife preserve with guided nature walks.

One native sport takes place in the scenic Tidal Basin near the Jefferson Memorial, where hundreds of paddle-boating enthusiasts take to the water each day.

Garden lovers can do their strolling amidst the blooming acres of the National Arboretum. Famed for the springtime display of the hillside planted with hybrid azaleas, the Arboretum also boasts prize herb and rose gardens, an impressive collection of boxwood, daylilies, daffodils, and dozens of other blooms that put on a show almost year round. There is also a prize collection of bonzai plants.

151

Above: *its bulbous shadow belying its sleek shape, the President's private plane awaits its V.I.P. passenger.*

Above: *a chauffeur awaits his employer beside a limousine, a common sight in this city of politicians.*

Right: *a Presidential motorcade stops the traffic in central Washington as the President returns home.*

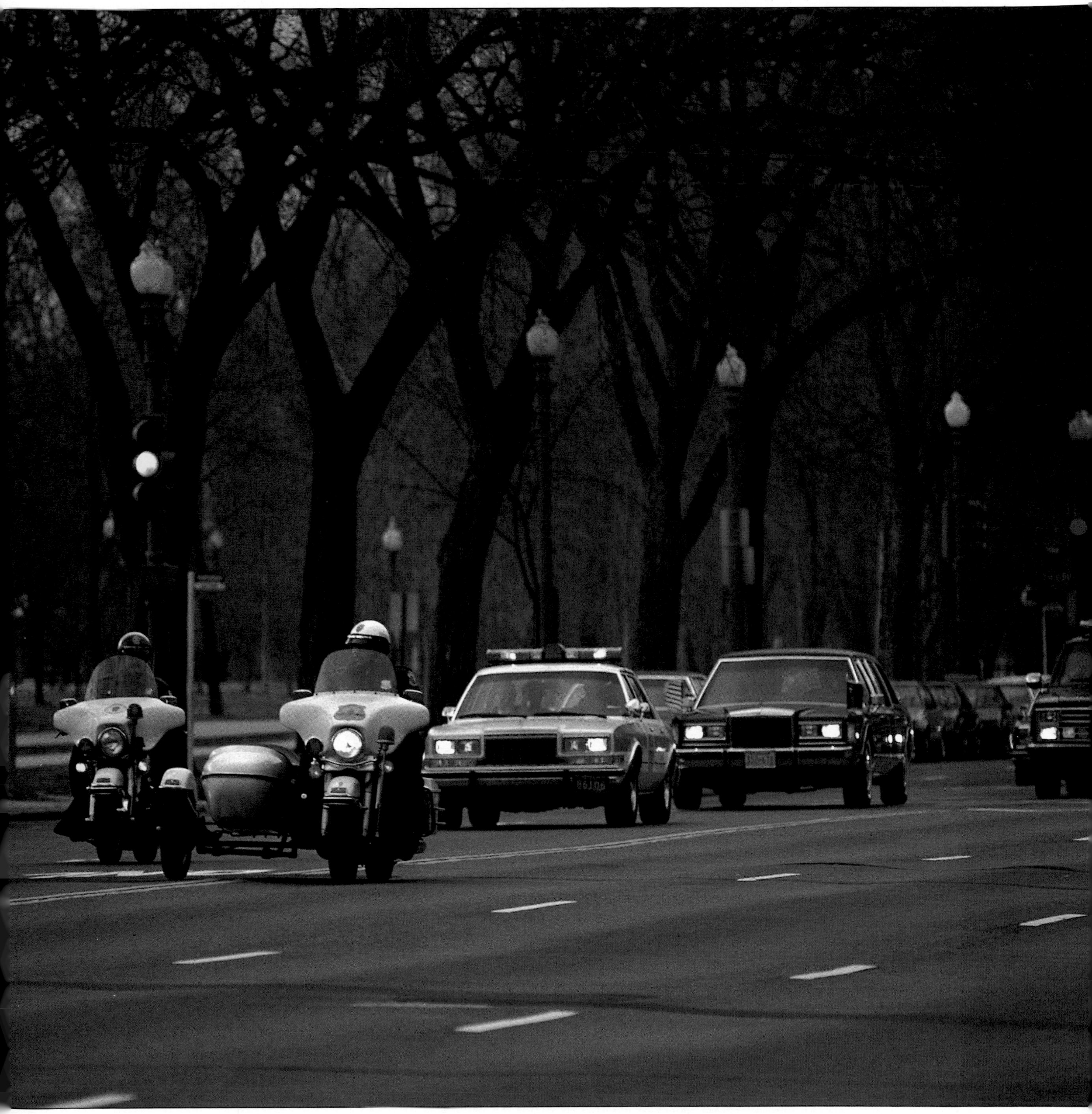

Above: *Fleetwood High School Marching Unit parades on the steps of the Capitol at a Presidential Inauguration.*

Right: *immaculate, perfectly matched, Budweiser drayhorses pull a beer wagon through the capital's streets.*

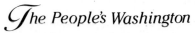

Right: *a sightseer provides herself with a clear view of the action at President Reagan's Inauguration in 1981.*

Above: *Sergeant Torres of the Airborne, a parachute regiment, on duty at President Reagan's Inauguration.*

Above: *crowds greet the American hostages back from Iran in 1981.*

Left: *an escort of police motorcyclists heralds the arrival of the President's limousine.*

Above: *an attentive crowd listens to President Reagan's Inaugural Address on the steps of the Capitol, January 1981.*

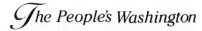

Above: *their blankets on the ground, crowds enjoy July 4 celebrations.*

Left: *perfect in pink, a little girl stands on the very edge of the Reflecting Pool on the Mall, the better to admire the ducks.*

Above: *pigeons, for all their destructive ways, are still regarded with affection by many Washingtonians.*

The People's Washington

Facing page: *in a packed stadium, Georgetown University basketball players confront Syracuse.*

Above: *a dramatic duet forms part of a modern dance rehearsal at Georgetown University.*

Left: *students study in the sun as an Indian summer day makes a bright start to the fall term at Georgetown University.*

Above: *flowers bloom and a student reads amid the gray Victorian stonework of Georgetown University.*

Left: *a shower of blossom encroaches upon a rain-sodden sidewalk at Georgetown University in spring.*

Facing page: *the U.S. Botanic Gardens, a tropical greenhouse that provides plants for Congressional offices.*

Above: *a degree and an engagement ring – the culmination of this student's career at Georgetown.*

Above: *Georgetown Park, an elegant Georgetown mall boasting wrought iron Victorian filigree and real plants.*

Right: *a house and pool on Hickory Hill, reminiscent in its luxury of the set of* The Philadelphia Story.

Above: *passengers await a flight to Los Angeles under the distinctively dipped roof of Washington's Dulles Airport.*

Right: *the writhing freeway complex beside the Pentagon, popularly known by the locals as "the Mixing Bowl."*

*Like raindrops sparkling in the sun on some great curling plant stem,
cars catch the summer morning light as they approach Dulles Airport.*

Above: *an office block's lights blaze cheerfully through a lacework of trees on a winter's night in downtown Washington.*
Right: *floodlit, the Capitol's dome shines over a darkened city.*

Washington by Night

Though best known for its political dramas, Washington in recent years has acquired a national reputation for culture, particularly theater. The Kennedy Center is the major key to this renaissance, but D.C. also has its share of innovative small theaters, and concerts are legion, ranging from the National Symphony to free outdoor concerts by the Army, Navy, and Marine bands.

The Kennedy Center

The city came into its own as a cultural center with the building of the John F. Kennedy Center for the Performing Arts. The Kennedy Center is unique in that it is both an arts center and a presidential memorial. The 100-foot-high grand foyer of the Edward Durell Stone building contains a fine Robert Berks bust of John F. Kennedy. The elegant building also includes a Hall of States and a Hall of Nations. The main arenas – the Eisenhower Theater, Opera House, and Concert Hall – have been embellished with gifts from many nations. Canada, Cyprus, Egypt, Mexico, Austria, France, Iran, Ireland, Sri Lanka, Argentina, Denmark, Great Britain, Israel, Norway, Switzerland, and twenty-two African nations are among those contributing to the decor. The Terrace Theater on the

Above: *ornate lampposts decorate the Capitol's steps.*

roof terrace level of the center was made possible by a three-million-dollar Bicentennial gift from the people and the government of Japan. The five hundred-seat house is an ideal setting for chamber music and recitals.

President Eisenhower took the first step toward an arts venue in 1955 when he appointed a commission to examine the feasibility of a national cultural center. In 1958, he signed the National Cultural Center Act into law and private fund-raising began for what was to be an independent, self-sustaining performing arts arena. In 1964, a unanimous joint resolution of Congress dedicated the center as the sole memorial in the nation's capital to the slain president. That same act authorized twenty-three million dollars in federal matching funds and borrowing authority to help the construction of the building to become a reality. Another thirty-four million dollars was quickly raised in private funds from donors wishing to honor John Kennedy.

Since the Kennedy Center opened its doors in 1971, it has operated 7 days a week, 365 days a year, and has welcomed more than sixty-five million visitors from every part of the United States and the world. With its colorful flags, Waterford crystal chandeliers, and spacious terraces on the Potomac, the Center is grand indeed, but the primary function here is to encourage the performing arts, and it does this admirably with six theaters seating from 2,759 to 120. The various arenas accommodate dance, drama, musical theater, classical and contemporary music and opera, theater, and film.

The Center is home to the National Symphony Orchestra, as well as the Washington Opera and the Washington Performing Arts Society. It is also a

Above: *Dulles International Airport, designed by Eero Saarinen, who thought it "the best he had ever done."*

Right: *foreshortening in a night shot contrives to bring the Washington Monument to the foot of the Capitol's steps.*

showcase for the world's outstanding performing artists, and it serves Americans across the country with radio and television programs, touring productions, and its education and public service programs. Much of this outreach is underwritten by the Corporate Fund, representing some four hundred American corporations.

The Theater Lab offers children's performances, teachers' workshops, and exhibits – all free or at low cost. The American Film Institute brings more than six hundred films and one hundred thousand movie-goers to the center each year. A reduced price ticket

program also helps ensure access to senior citizens, students, military personnel, and persons with disabilities. Each year more than five hundred thousand people attend these free and modestly priced events at the center.

The Center funds and fosters the creation of many new works in all the arts, and encourages young and lesser-known artists by giving them opportunities to perform and, through national competitions, to gain recognition. The contributions of outstanding performing artists to the nation's cultural life are also saluted at the annual Kennedy Center Honors gala, an

event that is televised to the entire country. The Kennedy Center Friedheim Awards program is the only significant national competition for original American music. Finalists perform at a free concert at the Center.

Other Leading Theaters

Another memorial to a tragic and historic assassination is Ford's Theatre, where Abraham Lincoln was felled by a bullet on April 14, 1864. The 741-seat theater has been authentically restored and

is once again home to live performances, including its own American, family-oriented plays and musicals. A basement museum contains memorabilia of the sad event of 1864.

The resident company that has brought Washington to the forefront of the country's regional theater movement is the Tony-Award-winning Arena Stage, a 35-year-old troupe located near the waterfront. The complex is actually three theaters, the in-the-round Arena seating 827, the smaller Kreeger Theater, and the underground Old Vat Room where Stephen Wade's *Banjo Dancing* is permanently ensconced.

The National Theatre, another local landmark and the oldest theater in continuous operation in the U.S., has also been lavishly restored and is now managed by Broadway's Schubert Organization, bringing Washington the pick of touring plays as well as many tryouts of new productions before they make it to New York. There are dozens of other theaters in the capital, from the Shakespeare Theatre at the Folger, an Elizabethan gem presenting classical drama, to the American Playwrights Theatre devoted to brand new works that showcase fresh talent.

Capital Nightlife

The night scene in the nation's capital reflects the diversity of people who live here – students, gays, Africans, Asians, Latin Americans, and middle Americans. In Washington at night you can dance a jig, join a square dance, take the mike at a comedy club, or sing along at a Japanese karaoke bar. Georgetown still has its share of nighttime fun, but Adams-Morgan is the hot spot, and the new downtown near the old theater district is picking up steam.

Dining out is a major Washington pastime, and no wonder, with cuisines from Afghan to Vietnamese to choose among. At least fifty nationalities are represented on the capital's menus.

But the truth is, on a fine night, Washingtonians need not head for a restaurant or a club or a concert hall to enjoy themselves. They can stroll up to the Capitol grounds, spread a picnic on the grass and listen to the Army, Navy, Air Force, or Marine Bands in free concerts – or wander over to the Marine Corps Barracks for the weekly sunset parade, complete with drum and bugle corps, silent drill teams, and saluting trumpeters.

Right: stalwart soldier holds aloft the United States flag as the sun sets on Veterans Day at the Tomb of the Unknown Soldier, Arlington Cemetery. Veterans Day falls annually on November 11.

Traffic streams through the
night in downtown
Georgetown, which some claim
to be the heart of Washington.

A soldier holds his rifle in
salute to a gold-fringed Old
Glory on Veterans Day at the
Tomb of the Unknown Soldier.

Or simply walk to the top of the steps of the Capitol or the Lincoln Memorial to look out at the Mall and the monuments bathed in floodlights, softly gleaming in the reflecting pools. It is one of the most memorable views on earth.

Such are the benefits of everyday life in the nation's capital. Over a century ago, historian Henry Adams wrote, "One of these days, this will be a very great city – if nothing happens to it." Much has happened – but all of it has helped make Adams's prediction come true.

Above: *a still winter's night in Washington – not even a faint ripple mars the reflection of the United States Capitol.*

Right: *the greatest of the capital's sights – the Lincoln Memorial, the Washington Monument and the Capitol.*